PRIVATE SELVES
PUBLIC IDENTITIES

PRIVATE SELVES

PUBLIC IDENTITIES

Reconsidering Identity Politics

SUSAN J. HEKMAN

THE PENNSYLVANIA STATE UNIVERSITY PRESS
UNIVERSITY PARK, PENNSYLVANIA

Library of Congress Cataloging-in-Publication Data

Hekman, Susan J.
    Private selves, public identities : reconsidering identity politics /
    Susan J. Hekman.
        p.   cm.
Includes bibliographical references and index.
ISBN 0-271-02382-1 (alk. paper)
    1. Privacy, Right of—United States.
    2. Politicians—United States.
    I. Title.

JC596.2. U5H45   2004
323'.01—dc22   2003022851

It is the policy of The Pennsylvania State University Press
to use acid-free paper. Publications on uncoated stock
satisfy the minimum requirements of American National
Standard for Information Sciences—Permanence of Paper
for Printed Library Material, ANSI Z39.48-1992.

CONTENTS

For Cecily

ACKNOWLEDGMENTS

This book began when I was on a fellowship at the Australian National University and Preston King invited me to edit a book on identity and difference. Having just finished a book on difference, I thought that identity would be the next logical step and accepted the invitation. It was and is, but I had no idea what I was getting into by taking on the question of identity. Identity is everywhere; it affects everything. The questions it raises almost invariably spiral out of control. Every attempt I made to get a handle on it only resulted in the generation of more questions. Identity is a crucial issue, both politically and personally. It is also one of the most difficult.

I published an early version of Chapter 1 in *Feminist Theory* in 2000. It is indicative of the struggles I have had with identity that in this article I came to a conclusion that is the opposite of what I come to here. I have asked for and received much help in these struggles. My greatest debt is to Nancy Hirschmann, who read early versions of the argument and helped me see more clearly what I was doing. Dick Flathman also read a draft of the manuscript and guided me through the complexities of contemporary liberalism. Mary Hawkesworth's and Eloise Buker's reviews pointed out weaknesses in the final argument. My thanks to all of you. And, as always, my deepest thanks to Buzz.

1

Constructing Identity

Questions of identity pervade nearly every aspect of contemporary life. Politicians debate the role of identity in the political sphere. Social and political theorists debate its theoretical status. Psychologists discuss competing theories of identity and
subjectivity. Popular books invite us to create and re-create our
identities on a daily basis, crafting new identities as the situation
demands. Most of these discussions, furthermore, revolve around
"solutions" to the "problem" of identity. The advocates of identity politics embrace it as a permanent and positive feature of
our political life. They champion the advent of different political identities, particularly those defined in terms of race and ethnicity. "We are all multiculturalists now," Nathan Glazer (1997)
asserts. Social, political, and psychological theorists each have a
particular position to argue on the question of identity and identity politics; each asserts that this position is the definitive solution to the problems raised by identity. Those who do not read
their often esoteric books are given equally definitive formulations by more popular authors.

Yet the problem of identity will not go away. None of the solutions that have been offered have been embraced by all parties; no one approach to identity solves all the issues raised. On

one level this is to be expected. Given the difficulty and breadth of the issues that identity raises, it is not surprising that an easy resolution of these issues cannot be found. In the following, I will break from the tradition of writings on identity and *not* claim that I have found the solution to the problem. On the contrary, I will argue that the problem of identity will not go away because contemporary issues of identity are too complex to be easily resolved. More specifically, I will argue that these issues challenge some of the basic presuppositions of our philosophical and political beliefs. The issues of identity cannot be "solved," in other words, because they challenge assumptions that are deeply ingrained in our social fabric. We need to uncover those assumptions before we can assess the impact of the debate over identity.

My intent here, then, is not to propose a solution to the problem of identity and identity politics but, rather, to develop a perspective on identity that reveals what is at stake in these debates. That perspective is informed by feminist theory and practice. Although issues of identity are not strictly feminist issues, I ground my argument in feminist discussions of identity for a number of reasons. First, the postmodern challenge to the modernist conception of identity developed by feminist theorists such as Judith Butler has been immensely influential in discussions of identity. Butler's fictive, inessential subject dramatically reveals the liabilities of the modernist subject. Although other challenges to this subject have been posed, the feminist argument has a particular resonance because it focuses on the masculinity of this subject. Understanding what is wrong, and right, about this conception is a necessary starting point for developing a new perspective on identity issues.

My second reason for focusing on feminism is that the feminist experience of identity politics offers the clearest illustration of the dilemma created by introducing identity into the liberal polity. Identity politics has perpetuated a debate in the feminist community that appears to have no resolution. Both embracing and rejecting the identity "woman" have unacceptable consequences for feminist theory and practice. Within the liberal polity as it is presently constituted, feminists and other marginalized groups can be neither for nor against identity.

My third reason is that feminist theorists have developed a critique of liberalism that reveals why identity politics is profoundly incompatible with the liberal polity. Explorations of why the identity "woman" has not fit neatly into liberal politics even after women's suffrage have led feminist theorists to a broader understanding of the role of identity in the liberal polity. Although this feminist critique has not been explicitly applied to the question of identity politics, I will argue that it can illuminate that discussion in significant ways. My strategy is to use this critique to question the relationship between identity and politics in the liberal tradition and suggest an alternative to that relationship.

Identity/Politics in Contemporary Feminism

In an influential article published in *Signs* in 1988, Linda Alcoff wrote: "For many contemporary feminist theorists, the concept of woman is a problem. It is a problem of primary significance because the concept of woman is the central concept for feminist theory. Yet it is a concept that is impossible to formulate precisely for feminists" (1988, 405). The context of Alcoff's argument was the widespread conviction among feminist theorists that the modernist conception of the self/individual that has dominated Western thought since the Enlightenment is inappropriate to women. The argument that this rational, disembodied subject is inherently masculine and thus defines women as inferior was nearly universally accepted by feminists at the time Alcoff was writing. The problem Alcoff is addressing in her article, however, is not the rejection of this concept but what might replace it. Although the rejection, either wholly or in part, was widely accepted, its replacement was the subject of heated debate.

Alcoff labels this situation the "identity crisis" in feminist theory. She argues that how the question of the concept of woman is resolved will profoundly affect the future of feminism, that it will define the identity of feminism by defining the identity of "woman." Alcoff is writing at the end of a decade in which one resolution of this crisis was dominant: the assertion of a monolithic concept of "woman" wholly different from that of "man." Identified with theorists such as Nancy Chodorow and Carol Gilligan "difference feminism" focused on the qualities shared by all women and, most notably, asserted that the alleged deficiencies of women are in fact virtues.[1]

By 1988 the critics of difference feminism had revealed serious liabilities in this conception. The most telling criticism was that difference feminism replicated the essentialist fixing of identity that was the hallmark of the modernist conception. Thus, like the modernist subject, it necessarily created a hierarchy within the category "woman" in which some women, white, middle-class, heterosexual women, were more "woman" than others. Differences between women were ignored or erased. Increasing emphasis on the diversity and complexity of actual women, however, made it difficult to construct arguments for the alleged universal characteristics of women's experiences. For all these rea-

---

1. I will argue later that such interpretations are misleading.

sons, Alcoff, along with many other feminist theorists, rejected difference feminism as a viable solution to the identity crisis in feminism.

The second possible resolution of the crisis was, in 1988, in the ascendancy: postmodernism/poststructuralism. Alcoff defines this position as the claim that "woman" cannot be defined and any attempt to do so is misguided. Alcoff has problems with this alternative as well. She claims that its nominalism reduces the category of "woman" to a fiction, and that this will lead to a wholly negative feminism (1988, 417–18). Alcoff's rejection of both these alternatives leads her to advocate what she calls a "third way," a definition of gendered identity as positionality. The third way is a kind of hybrid in the sense that it combines elements of both the opposing conceptions. It preserves the agency of the modernist subject and grafts this onto the discursive construction of the poststructuralist subject. In Alcoff's view her position integrates the best elements of both conceptions.

I am beginning my story about identity and identity politics with Alcoff's article because it outlines the context that frames the debate in which feminism is now embroiled. Alcoff's reservations about the poststructuralist/postmodernist conception of the subject did not go away. On the contrary, they continued to appear in the debate over identity and identity politics throughout the 1990s. The question of how we can have feminist politics without the concept "woman" is never satisfactorily answered for many feminists. What Alcoff did not foresee, however, was the strength of the postmodern position that she rejects. Two years after her article was published, Judith Butler's *Gender Trouble* (1990) revolutionized the debate over identity and identity politics. Despite the widespread reservations of critics such as Alcoff, Butler's position enjoyed immense popularity because it seemed to offer precisely the solution that feminism was seeking. Butler definitely rejects the essential identity of the modernist tradition and offers a radical alternative: woman as fiction. Butler's position, more than any other feminist alternative, set the stage for subsequent discussions of identity and identity politics.

Alcoff, at the end of her article, briefly takes up the question of identity politics. She argues that identity politics provides a counter to the "disembodied individual" of liberal theory and, most notably, problematizes the connection of identity and politics by revealing the constructed nature of identity (1988, 433). In light of the debate over the following decade, this statement is difficult to assess. On the one hand, it is abundantly obvious that identity politics has not resulted in the problematizing of identity or the revelation of the constructed nature of identity but, rather, has moved to fix identity in new locations. Identity politics has introduced a plethora of identities in the political sphere. But on the other hand, these identities have not been conceptualized as the fluid, unstable identities that Alcoff, and certainly Butler, define. Rather, the new identities in the political arena are conceived as fixed and monolithic. The members of identity groups feel forced to conform to a rigidly defined identity. This fixing tendency has become the basis of many of the criticisms of identity politics, particularly in the feminist community. Alcoff's conviction that identity politics would problematize the relationship between identity and politics thus has not materialized. But Alcoff was right to assert that it has the potential to do so. Realizing this potential, however, necessitates much more radical change than Alcoff imagined. It entails calling into question the philosophical and political foundation of the liberal polity. The practice of identity politics is radical, but in ways that were not immediately obvious at the time of Alcoff's article.

The strands of meaning embedded in the issues of identity and identity politics are difficult to unravel. In what follows I will return to many of the issues mentioned above and introduce others. Overall, however, my thesis is that the discussion of identity and identity politics in feminist theory, as well as that of social and political theory more generally, rests on three fundamental misconceptions. The first involves a misunderstanding of personal identity. In the rush to reject the modernist, abstract, disembodied subject of the Enlightenment tradition, the appeal of the postmodern subject, particularly as it has been elaborated by Butler, was overwhelming. Despite the reservations about the fictive subject in the feminist community, Butler's postmodern subject has had immense influence in discussions of identity and identity politics. The assumption informing these discussions is that unless we completely jettison the notion of a coherent identity that is associated with the modernist subject, we will continue to be caught in its evident errors. In other words, these discussions assume that unless we accept the fictive subject, the only alternative is the modernist subject. Attempts by theorists such as Alcoff to combine incompatible elements of the modernist and discursive subject are evidence of the dilemma caused by this assumption.

My argument is that the fictive subject of Butler's theory is not the only alternative to the modernist subject. We do not, as Butler claims, reinvent ourselves every day, performing the actions that constitute our identity. Nor are we wholly formed by the hegemonic discourses that constitute our society; we are not social dupes. Rather, each of us possesses a coherent, core self that allows us to function as mature adults in a social world and provides us with an individual identity. But we need not assume that this core self is essential, disembodied, or abstract, a version of the modernist subject. Rather, it is itself socially constituted in the early years of childhood. To make this argument I will turn to a theory that recently has been much maligned in the feminist community, object relations theory. My claim it that object relations theory can be reinterpreted to theorize the subject as what I call an "ungrounded ground." I argue that we all possess, by necessity, a core self but that this self is a social product constituted by a complex array of forces that are both public and personal.

The second misconception informing discussions of identity and identity politics involves the role of identity in the liberal polity. Since the advent of liberalism in the seventeenth century, we have been told that identity does not belong in the political arena. The citizen of the liberal polity is, like the modernist subject, abstract and disembodied. His [sic] personal concerns and identity are not relevant to his public political self. This conception of the citizen is what makes identity politics fundamentally illegitimate in the liberal polity. Since identities do not belong in the political arena, those who enter the public sphere embodying such identities, women, blacks, gays, and so on, find that they do not belong; they are segregated as "others." These others are opposed to the allegedly neutral citizen who lacks an identity.

Except that he does not. As feminist critics such as Carole Pateman have revealed, the citizen of the liberal polity possesses a very distinct identity: the white, male property owner of the liberal tradition. The problems created by this citizen have a direct bearing on identity politics. The identity of the citizen in the liberal polity is veiled by the ideology of the abstract citizen. This veiling creates a paradoxical situation: the identity of the abstract citizen is both present and absent in the liberal polity. It is present in the sense that it is the contrast to this citizen that defines the others precisely *as* others. It is absent in the sense that his identity is never acknowledged *as* an identity. The result is that identity politics is doomed to failure in the liberal polity. Because the identity of the abstract citizen is never acknowledged, it is never possible to legitimate "other" identities.

My argument is that if we strip away the veil hiding the abstract citizen, exposing the fallacy of the concept, radical consequences follow. If politics is and has always been about identities, then they are not illegitimate aspects of politics, but, rather, necessary elements. If there is no abstract citizen, then the goal of subsuming all differences under a generic concept is revealed as meaningless and counterproductive. It entails that dealing with differences between citizens is not an aberration to be avoided at all costs but a necessary and legitimate element of political life. What is entailed, in short, is a very different politics, a politics that constitutes a radical departure from liberalism.

The third misconception inherent in discussions of identity and identity politics involves the failure to distinguish between personal and public identity. One of the principal criticisms of identity politics is that it necessarily involves the fixing of identity in a particular location. To engage, for example, in lesbian identity politics is to fix one's identity as the "Lesbian," an identity that allows for no ambiguity or differences between individual lesbians (Phelan 1989). It also forces lesbians to choose their sexual orientation as the essence of their identity, denying all other aspects of that identity. All of us have multiple aspects to our identity. Identity politics as it is now constituted forces us to choose one of those aspects as our essential identity.

My argument is that this is a false dilemma. *Identity* has been made to do too much work in our vocabularies. Each of us possesses a personal identity that is constituted by an array of influences and experiences that form us as a unique person. These forces are both public, the hegemonic discourses that define our social life, and individual, the character and situation of those who care for us as infants and through whom the public concepts are transmitted to us. The result of these influences is what I have referred to above as our core self. But in addition to possessing a personal identity, each of us is subsumed under an array of public identities: woman/man; white/nonwhite; middle class/working class, and so forth. Political action is one of the sites of interface between public and personal identity. When, for example, I enter the public arena espousing the identity "woman," I am acknowledging that I am subsumed under this public category. My political action entails that I *identify* with this category, but I do not and cannot bring all the aspects of my personal identity into that act of political identification. My personal identity is not fixed by the definition of "woman" that feminist politics represents. Rather, I am choosing a public, political identification that is rooted in my personal identity, an identity whose complexities exceed that identification.

The problem is that *identity* means, in our language, both difference and sameness. Our personal identity makes us different from everyone else. Our public identity identifies us as the same as particular others. My argument is that personal and public identities must be understood as different entities while it is still acknowledged that they interact in complex ways. The public, hegemonic identity of "woman" plays an integral part in forming the identity of every woman in this society. But every woman in this society is different. My socialization into the concept of "woman" will overlap with yours but not be identical to it. We are all embedded in social structures but our embeddedness occurs at different locations. Thus one of us rebels against the hegemonic concept "woman" and becomes a feminist and another conforms to that concept. We need a theory that can explain both these developments.

My discussion of these three misconceptions of identity and identity politics correspond roughly to the first three chapters of the book. I say roughly because it is difficult to separate the strands of the discussion. To say that identity is a complex issue is a vast understatement. The personal and political, individual and social, overlap in multiple ways, making clear distinctions difficult. Which is precisely the point. Neat, clear distinctions distort the complexity of the issues raised by the problem of identity. Identity must be understood from within that complexity, not through a denial of it.

Butler on Identity: Doers and Deeds

In the following chapter I will argue that the identity of the liberal citizen creates a dilemma not only for women but for all the "others" defined by the liberal polity. But the problem with identity is not restricted to the liberal citizen. It is a function of modernism itself and the abstract, disembodied subject that is its core. Attempts to formulate an alternative to the modernist subject have abounded in the twentieth century. I will focus here on one of those alternatives: the postmodern fictive subject as articulated by Judith Butler. I do so because Butler's theory has colored discussions of identity and identity politics both within and without the feminist community. Revealing the errors implicit in Butler's assumptions is necessary to a reassessment of the complex array of issues raised by identity.

Judith Butler's theory of identity has been at one and the same time the most influential and most criticized feminist theory of identity in the last decade. The 1990 publication of *Gender Trouble* changed the theoretical landscape of feminist discussions of identity. It now forms a kind of baseline from which all discussions of identity must begin. Even those who ultimately reject Butler's theory must begin the presentation of their own theories with an analysis of her approach.

The fundamental presupposition that informs Butler's argument in *Gender Trouble* is the bankruptcy of the modernist subject and all the qualities associated with it. The modernist subject, we have been told, is a stable entity, a coherent unity that makes agency possible. The subject acts from that coherent, stable core that constitutes personhood. Against this, Butler argues that there is no "abiding substance" that constitutes a person, but, rather, such a substance is a "fictive construct." Radical conclusions follow from this theory:

> If the notion of an abiding substance is a fictive construction produced through the compulsory ordering of attributes into coherent gender sequences, then it seems that gender as substance, the viability of *man* and *woman* as norms, is called into question by the dis-

sonant play of attributes that fail to conform to sequential or causal modes of intelligibility.

and

But if these substances are nothing other than the coherences contingently created through the regulation of attribute, it would seem that the ontology of substances itself is not only an artificial effect but essentially superfluous. (1990, 24)

Butler is applying a strategy here that will inform her argument throughout the book: claiming that what something seems to be is actually its opposite. While we had thought that our gender identity produces the expressions of gender, she is claiming that the opposite is true: "There is no gender identity behind the expressions of gender; that identity is performatively constituted by the very 'expressions' that are said to be its results" (1990, 25). Thus gender identity *is* its acts; without the acts there would be no gender (140). It follows that "[g]ender ought not to be considered as a stable identity or locus of agency from which various acts follow; rather, gender is an identity tenuously constituted in time, instituted in an exterior space through a *stylized repetition of acts*" (140; Butler's emphasis).

The ontological "mistake" of gender identity, however, is only one of the problems with the concept. The assumption that a stable, coherent gender identity precedes and makes possible any conceivable action effectively hides the actions that, in Butler's theory, constitute gender. As she puts it, the "political regulations and disciplinary practices" that produce what we call gender identity are hidden from view precisely because they are defined as effects rather than constitutive elements (136). Butler wants to correct this with what she calls a "political genealogy of gender" that will "expose the contingent acts that create the appearance of a naturalistic necessity" (33).

The now (in)famous conclusion that Butler draws from all this is that gender is "performative" (25). It is the *performing* of gender that constitutes gender identity, not a pregiven essence: "That the gendered body is performative suggests that is has no ontological status apart from the various acts which constitute its reality" (136). But Butler's theory of performativity (as it will later be called) does more than jettison the modernist subject. It also necessitates and defines a particular form of resistance. If performances in accordance with gender ideology constitute gender identity, then any actions that do not conform to this ideology subvert it. The concept here is very straightforward: we subvert gender identity by acting in ways that do not conform to gender identity. The theme of subversive acts is repeatedly addressed in *Gender Trouble*. But although the theory behind Butler's concept of subversion is straightforward, the practice is not. It is significant that Butler's references to subversive acts almost always appear in the form of questions: How can we identify *which* acts will be subversive? How can we locate subversive strategies? (31–32, 147). Butler's answer to these questions is also significant in that it is decidedly vague. We are told that subversive acts should take the form of pastiche. She goes on to carefully distinguish pastiche from parody, the mocking of an original, because, she claims, there is no original gender identity to mock (146). Neither pastiche nor parody, however, are given any concrete political description.

What Butler is very clear about, however, is the implication of her argument for identity politics. The identity "woman" that informs much feminist politics is just as foundational as what it seeks to replace and thus cannot be transformative (15). What we need instead is an "open coalition" that "affirms identities that are alternatively instituted and relinquished according to the purposes at hand" (16). In other words, Butler argues that the identity "woman" cannot be the presupposition of a feminist politics, but, rather, the *doing* of identity politics will create the identities that it enacts (142). The result, Butler claims, will not be the deconstruction of politics or identity, but rather will establish as political the very terms through which identity is articulated (149).

Gender Trouble hit the feminist community like a storm. Accolades and criticisms poured out in journals and books. In 1993 Butler published *Bodies That Matter* in part as "a rethinking of some parts of *Gender Trouble* that have caused confusion" (1993, xii). Two themes dominate her discussion here that also figured prominently in *Gender Trouble*. First, identity as a fiction, the startling thesis of *Gender Trouble*, is now refined as "a process of iterability," a "constrained repetition of norms" (1993, 95). Many critiques of *Gender Trouble* focused on Butler's definition of the subject as free play. Butler now argues that identity is not a fiction in the sense that it is created anew every morning. But it is a fiction in that there is no essence that produces actions. It is the repetition of norms, rather, that enable and constitute the subject.

The second theme is subversion, resistance. Butler now admits that *Gender Trouble*'s advocacy of pastiche as a political strategy was too vague. "The task now," she asserts, "is to refigure this necessary 'outside' as a future horizon, one in which the violence of exclusion is perpetually in the process of being overcome" (53). But once again Butler cautions that identity politics will not accomplish this goal, because it holds out the promise of unity that will always be disappointed. "How," Butler asks, "might the excluded return, not as psychosis or the figure of the psychotic within politics, but as that which has been rendered mute, foreclosed from the domain of political signification?" (189). The context of Butler's remark here is a long and ultimately critical analysis of Žižek's call for a political performative that will produce temporary linguistic unity. But Butler rejects even this temporary unity. "Woman," she insists, must be a permanent site of contest; there should not be even temporary closure (221).

If identity politics as we know it is ineffectual and even a temporary unity is rejected, where does this leave us? Butler argues that it is in the performative itself that we can discover the possibility of subversion. The performative, she claims, can produce a set of consequences that exceed and confound the disciplinary intentions of the law: "It is the constitutive failure of the performative, this slippage between discursive command and its appropriated effect, that provides the linguistic occasion and index for a consequential disobedience (122).

Identifying subversive action and defining strategies of resistance is a much more prominent theme of *Bodies That Matter* than of *Gender Trouble*. Two factors structure Butler's argument. First, she must demonstrate that the rejection of the modernist subject does not entail the denial of agency. She must demonstrate, in other words, that the discursively constituted subject she is describing can act, and, most important, resist. Second, she must avoid the error of opposition, that is, crafting strategies of subversion/resistance that are the precise opposite of the hegemonic ideology that we seek to subvert. She argues that adopting an oppositional strategy entails that we are as much in thrall to that ideology as those who conform to it.

Butler's solution to both problems is what she calls "incoherent identities." "Identifications," she asserts, "are never fully and finally made; they are subject to the volatile logic of iterability" (1993, 105). Against the proponents of identity politics she argues that what we need is the "political resistance of incoherent identities" (115). Coherent identities are dangerous. They are a throwback to the modernist subject, replicating the fixed identity that is the hallmark of that subject. A corollary of Butler's position here is one that will become a major theme of the critics of identity politics: insisting on coherent identities results in the policing of identities (117). Fixed identities, in other words, are always coercive.

Despite her rejection of both oppositional strategies and fixing identities, Butler is nevertheless aware of the appeal of these positions. She even concedes that it is at times necessary to assert political demands through recourse to identity categories (227). But she also asserts that this cannot be a long-term strategy. Rather than succumbing to the temptation of asserting coherent identities, we must instead take stock of the "constitutive exclusions that reconsolidate hegemonic power differentials" lest we "replicate at the level of identity politics the very exclusionary morass that initiated the turn to specific identities in the first place" (118).

It is important to keep in mind that one of Butler's principal goals in *Bodies That Matter* was to clarify the vague political prescriptions of *Gender Trouble* and formulate a political strategy that is compatible with performativity. It is fair to ask, then, whether she has accomplished this goal. The answer must be a definitive no. Exactly what her incoherent identities are to do politically is just as unclear at the end of *Bodies That Matter* as it was at the beginning. She has told us that her task is to "refigure this necessary 'outside' as a future horizon" (53), but she has not even outlined how this task might be accomplished. At the end of the book Butler seems to concede this when she asks, "How will we know the difference between the power we promote and the power we oppose?" (241).

It is significant that once more Butler moves on to a new book to answer a question left hanging in her previous book. But while the goal of *Bodies That Matter* was to clarify the political strategy of *Gender Trouble*, the goal of Butler's 1997 book, *Excitable Speech: A Politics of the Performative*, is to illustrate how difficult it is to develop such a political strategy. The title of this book leads the reader to hope for a continuation of the discussion in *Bodies That Matter* on the possibilities of a nonidentity politics. It is this, but rather than clarify the issues raised in the previous book it offers more complications. The topic of the book is hate speech, and the argument that Butler advances is clear: laws against hate speech are ineffectual. Butler's argument is that language names us, calls us into social existence—and thus, defining a particular kind of naming, for example, racial invective, as inherently injurious, misunderstands the function of language. For certain words to constitute harm, certain conditions must prevail; it is not possible to simply inspect words in order to decide what is a threat (1997a, 13). *Queer* can be injurious, congratulatory, or humorous, depending on the context. Hate speech exposes a prior vulnerability to language, but we are all vulnerable to language in myriad ways; a specific vulnerability cannot be set apart by law. Another way of putting this is that hate speech always takes place in the context of history. Prosecuting it effectively would entail prosecuting all of our history (50).

In Chapter 4, I will make an argument that parallels Butler's here. My point, like hers, is that a strictly political solution, for example, passing laws outlawing hate speech, is insufficient. The problem is deeper, embedded in the social fabric that constitutes our history. The point I want to make here, however, is a different one. Butler is rejecting a clear-cut strategy of resistance—outlawing hate speech—without formulating a viable alternative. The "politics of the performative" promised in the title comes to this:

> The word that wounds becomes an instrument of resistance in the redeployment that destroys the prior territory of its operation. Such a redeployment means speaking words without prior authorization and putting into risk the security of linguistic life, the sense of one's place in language, that one's words do as one says. . . . Insurrectionary speech becomes the necessary response to injurious language, a risk taken in response to being put at risk, a repetition in language that forces change. (163)

Once more we are left without the political strategy that we have been promised.[2]

In my attempt to assess Butler's theory of identity, I want to do more than add to the now formidable literature criticizing her concept. These criticisms have been largely ineffectual; articulating yet another critique would probably not change the situation. In order to avoid this, then, I will begin by examining why Butler's theory has had such an immense impact. Why, despite the extensive critiques of Butler's concept of the subject, does it continue to exert such influence? Butler must have done something right if her concept has shaped feminist discussions of identity for more than a decade. She must have struck a responsive chord in the feminist community.

What Butler did right, first, was to definitively reject the modernist subject. Other feminists, obviously, had also criticized this subject, but Butler's critique was effective because it put this critique in the context of issues that dominated feminist discussions in the 1990s: identity politics, the social production of gender, psychoanalysis, and difference. Butler's argument that "there is no there there" thus spoke to feminists in a way that previous critiques had not. Butler made it very clear that the modernist, essentialist subject must go if feminism is to succeed. The second thing that Butler did right was to focus on the social and political forces that produce gender. Again, although other feminists

---

2. William Connolly's position in *Identity/Difference* (1991) falls prey to many of the same problems I have identified in Butler. Like Butler, he jettisons the essentialist subject, replacing it with a subject that is "contingent and ambiguous." He rejects identity politics because it replicates the fixing of identity that he has repudiated, but the political strategy he advocates, like Butler's, is vague: an "ironic" political stance. Finally, like Butler, he concedes that some kind of core self may be necessary—he calls it a "dense self"—but he does no more than mention it in passing (1991, 64).

had theorized gender as a social construction, the radicalism of Butler's formulation gave the theory a new perspective. Butler's assertion that gender is, in a literal sense, the performance of gender took social determinism to a new level. Its very radicalness ensured its popularity.

Third, Butler's condemnation of identity politics came at a time when many feminists were questioning its viability. Elizabeth Spelman's *Inessential Woman: Problems of Exclusion in Feminist Thought* (1988), published right before *Gender Trouble*, spoke to many feminists' reservations about the concept "woman." Spelman's book articulated a widely shared belief that difference feminism resulted in the erasure of differences between women. *Gender Trouble* reinforced this belief. But, once again, Butler's position was the radical alternative, contributing to its appeal. Butler's forceful condemnation not only of the identity "woman" but also the identity politics to which it was linked was the right theory at the right time.

It is my contention that what Butler got right has stood in the way of seeing what she got wrong. Although Butler has been widely criticized, her theory has nevertheless enjoyed wide popularity because, on certain key issues, she articulated a theory appropriate to feminist concerns. But it is also my contention that unless we understand what is wrong with Butler's theory we cannot answer the questions she raises about identity and identity politics.

What Butler got wrong is the assumption that pervades her work: the conviction that all the attributes of the modernist subject must be rejected because embracing any of these attributes will incur all the dangers of that subject. The fictive subject, in other words, must have none of these attributes. There is a certain irony to this position. One of Butler's central themes is that opposites inhabit each other and thus that adopting an oppositional stance is a counterproductive strategy because opposites are a function of that which they oppose. Yet her theory of performativity constitutes such a strategy of opposition. Butler's thesis is that either we embrace the essentialist subject or we embrace nothing—a void that performs actions that constitute a fiction.

This fictive subject, to be fair, has been the source of many critiques of Butler's work. But I think that many of these critiques have been unsuccessful because they accept Butler's assumption that we must choose between essence and a void. Thus many of her critics, like Alcoff, feel compelled to return to the modernist subject in order to preserve qualities such as agency. In the following I will argue that Butler's position rests on a false opposition and that there is a viable alternative, what I call an ungrounded ground. Like many of Butler's critics I do not want to abandon social construction. But I also do not want to abandon the notion of a coherent self who acts from a stable core of identity. My thesis is that one can theorize a stable core of identity without abandoning social construction or presupposing an essential, pregiven subject, namely, the modernist subject or some version of it. Hence I argue for a core self that is socially constructed in the early years of childhood but nevertheless provides a secure base for the adult subject. It is a grounded, secure self, but the grounding is itself socially constructed.

There are indications that, on some level, Butler herself realizes the liability of the fictive subject. In one of the books that follows *Bodies That Matter*, *The Psychic Life of Power* (1997b), Butler turns away from the relatively practical problems of identity and identity politics to the realm of abstract theory. She continues to argue that we must reject any internal core of subjectivity. But she also concedes, although only in passing, that some version of such a core is necessary to psychic health. She argues that if children are to "persist in a psychic and social sense there must be dependency and the foundation of attachment: there is no possibility of not loving, where love is bound up with the requirements for life" (8). Further, in a discussion of the possibility of an ethical subject, Butler remarks that "we might reread 'being' as precisely the potentiality that remains unexhausted by any particular interpellation. Such a failure of interpellation may well undermine the capacity of the subject to 'be' in a self-identical sense, but it may also mark the path toward a more open, even more ethical kind of being, one of or for the future" (131). All of Butler's basic themes are here: the definition of resistance as the failure of subjectification; the denial of a "self-identical" subject. But there is also a new element: a "being" that escapes subjectification. What this being could consist of is a puzzle. It sounds curiously like an essential being, but obviously cannot be, because Butler has vehemently denied the existence of such an entity. I would like to suggest that Butler, in her obsessive desire to reject any possibility of an essential subject, is forced by the logic of her argument to fall back on precisely such a subject. In other words, Butler's advocacy of the polar opposite of the essential subject leads her back to some version of that subject.

Against Butler I will argue that we need a concept of a stable, coherent identity, but this need not entail a return to the essentialist, modernist subject. We can theorize a stable identity without abandoning our commitment to social construction. Without a coherent identity, actors cannot act; they require a stable sense of self to avoid the fragmentation and splintering that is the mark of insanity. In short, I will argue that Butler's fictive subject is not a necessary consequence of the rejection of the essentialist subject and, furthermore, not a viable conception.

Two aspects of Butler's subject in particular reveal its liability. The first is the concept of resistance/subversion that Butler describes for this subject. Butler tells us that resistance is pastiche, not parody, that it comes from the margins, from the spaces where identification fails. But Butler's question at the end of *Bodies That Matter* still haunts: how can we tell the difference between the power we promote and the power we oppose? It is unclear how the fictive, performative subject acts in the first place and, further, what actions she might perform and what power she might subvert. Even if we can follow Butler's convoluted pronouncements, there is no conceivable political strategy that emerges from them.

The second vulnerable aspect of Butler's subject is the centerpiece of her theory: rigid social determinism. If, as Butler claims, we are all products of the discourses that constitute us, how can we explain the differences between us, particularly between women who are, on her account, constituted by the hegemonic concept "woman"? Specifically, how do we explain the fact that some women resist and others conform? Butler addresses this issue, if she addresses it at all, by talking about "slippage," the space where identification fails and hence resistance is possible. This explanation is inadequate. Where does the slippage come from? Why does it affect some rather than others? Butler's theory fails to explain the differences in identities and actions that characterize any social situation. We are all determined to a certain extent by cultural forces, but this is only part of the story. A strict cultural determinist theory cannot explain the other parts of the story.

An adequate theory of identity must be able to explain how individual identities are formed. It must have an explanation for how hegemonic concepts such as "woman" are filtered through the lens of individual situations. It must explain how race, class, and ethnicity as well as the peculiarities of particular families shape identities not as identical but as different. It must be able to explain the intersection of public identities such as "woman," "middle class," "black," "Italian," and so on with the particulars of individual families and social situations and how these combine to construct a personal identity. Butler's theory accomplishes none of these tasks.[3]

Identity as Ungrounded Ground

Near the end of *Gender Trouble*, Butler summarizes her position by arguing that "gender identity might be reconceived as a personal/cultural history of received meanings subject to a set of initiative practices which refer laterally

---

3. Allison Weir's critique of Butler has some of the same elements as mine, particularly her argument that we must recognize differences between identities (1996). But Weir turns to Julia Kristeva for her reconstructed theory of identity, a move that I think compounds the problem.

to other imitations and which, jointly, construct the illusion of a primary and interior gendered self or parody the mechanism of that construction" (1990, 138). I have argued above that this conception of identity is flawed and that we need an alternative conception to negotiate the complexities of public and private identities. I will begin my advocacy of this alternative by describing the dangers of the fictive, ungrounded subject that Butler theorizes. Much has been written on the failure of Butler's concept from an epistemological perspective: the denial of the subject and agency. I will focus here on the psychological problems of the fictive self: the psychological danger of positing a subject without a coherent sense of self.

The literature on identity and identity politics has little to say about this danger. One of the few exceptions to this, James Glass's *Shattered Selves: Multiple Personality in a Postmodern World* (1993), is rarely cited in the debates that swirl around identity. Glass argues that the postmodern conception of self and identity is dangerous, because it posits the self as a rhetorical category, not a real, feeling, experiencing being. The most powerful critique of this concept, he argues, comes from the words and lives of individuals experiencing multiple personality disorder. His argument is directed specifically against the postmodern theorists who advocate a playful, "creative" approach to identity, and, most important, define schizophrenia and multiple personality disorder as liberatory deconstructions of identity. Against this Glass argues that fragmented, shattered identities are evidence of pain, not liberation. They are not playful, creative, or aesthetic. Commenting on one victim of multiple personalities, he asserts: "Hers is not a liberatory, playful experience; her multiple realities annihilate the self's emotional possibility, destroy the psychological foundations of consent, shatter the shared experiences of historical knowledge" (1993, 46).

Glass's conclusions are drawn from research he conducted on women suffering from schizophrenia and multiple personality disorder. The pain that these women suffer is palpable; the disorientation of their lives is difficult to read about, much less experience. Glass makes a strong case that the unity of the self is both a difficult achievement and a necessary requirement for leading any version of a good and satisfying life. A stable identity, he argues, is necessary because it "locates the self in the world; it defines emotional and interpersonal knowledge; it frames the self in a historical and situational context" (48). In clinical psychology, selves that lack coherence are problems, not solutions. Glass concludes that utilizing schizophrenia or other identity disorders as an ideal deconstructed identity is irresponsible and insensitive to the human costs of these illnesses. It is also condescending. Postmodern theorists are idealizing a structureless void that they will never have to experience. Nor will they, as therapists, have to repair the damage done to individuals who live in this condition.

In one respect Glass's critique is overblown and inaccurate. None of the post-moderns he discusses argue that we should literally become fragmented selves, that we should embrace schizophrenia. Gilles Deleuze and Felix Guattari (1977), the theorists most closely associated with the theory of schizophrenia, offer a convoluted argument in which schizophrenia becomes both the characteristic malady of capitalist society and the possibility of its revolution. Our society produces "schizos," they claim, like it produces Prell shampoo; capitalism both produces and necessarily inhibits schizophrenia. Deleuze and Guattari conclude that the schizo is not revolutionary, but the schizophrenic process is the potential of revolution (341). Likewise, Butler does not in a literal sense advocate that we all enact the fractured selves of schizophrenia in order to deconstruct hegemonic ideologies. The substanceless void of the subject that she theorizes is not the schizophrenic of psychoanalysis.[4]

But on another level, Glass's point is both valid and disturbing. His thesis is that selves must necessarily experience themselves as coherent entities, historically located and contingent, but enduring through time. This self allows subjects to place themselves in their historical context, to cope with the contingency of their existence. It is this self that is absent from Butler's discussion of identity and the self. Another critique of Butler from this perspective is that of Lynne Layton in *Who's That Boy? Who's That Girl? Clinical Practice Meets Postmodern Gender Theory* (1998). It is significant that this critique comes not from the mainstream of feminist theory but from the margins, from a practicing clinician attempting to grapple with the postmodern theory of identity in the therapeutic situation. Like Glass's book, it is rarely cited in identity debates. Layton attempts to reconcile postmodern identity theorists such as Butler with patients who claim to have a "core" identity and, most important, find that life without such an identity is untenable. Layton's problematic is her discovery that "there is a radical schism between postmodern celebrations of identity fluidity and what most people find it like to live an embodied, raced and gendered life in contemporary America" (25). Her goal is to bridge this gap, to employ the insights of postmodern theory regarding the cultural construction of gender without losing sight of the necessity of a core self and, particularly, a stable gender identity.

Layton's answer to her problem is object relations theory. She argues that object relations theory supplies a definition of a core self that is neither innate nor essential but relational. This core self provides the subject with a position

---

4. In *The Hysteric's Guide to the Future Female Subject* (2000), Juliet MacCannell argues that we should embrace hysteria as a guideline for the creation of a feminine subject and a feminine ethic. Unlike Butler, she appears to mean this quite literally.

in discourse from which negotiations can be made, but is itself a product of the subject's negotiations of early childhood relationships. As a clinician, Layton wants to use this concept of a core self to deal with two kinds of pain that she sees in her patients. First, she wants to deal with the pain experienced by subjects who suffer because they have rejected dominant gender norms. She wants to be able to explain how these subjects came to be gender rebels, and, most important, how to deal with their desire for the love and acceptance that has been denied them. Second, she wants to be able to deal with patients who lack a core self and, as a consequence, live a fragmented and tormented life. She notes: "In postmodern work that lauds indeterminacy, fragmentation is essentialized, universalized, and celebrated in a way that seems not to acknowledge what it feels like to experience it" (124).

To offer an example of a fragmented self in pain, Layton refers to Butler's analysis of Michel Foucault's *Herculine Barbin* (1980a). I would like to extend this analysis to reinforce the points I am making against Butler's concept of identity. The point of Butler's discussion is to fault Foucault for contradicting himself on the status of sexual pleasure. Foucault wants to argue that there is no "sex" itself, but that sex is produced by the complex interactions of discourse and power. Yet in *Herculine Barbin* Foucault seems to characterize Herculine's sexual pleasures as a result of his/her "happy limbo of non-identity" (Butler 1990, 100). Against Foucault, Butler argues that "the question of sexual difference re-emerges in a new light when we dispense with the metaphysical reification of multiplicitous sexuality and inquire in the case of Herculine into the concrete narrative structures and political and cultural conventions that produce and regulate the tender kisses, the diffuse pleasures, and the thwarted and transgressive thrills of Herculine's sexual world" (98).

Butler has undoubtedly scored a point against Foucault here. Herculine's deviant sexuality, like that of normative sexuality, is produced and regulated by the law of sex. What is glaringly absent in both accounts, however, is any reference to Herculine's pain, or, indeed, his/her eventual suicide. Both Butler and Foucault are so concerned with probing the discursive construction of Herculine's sexuality that they overlook this pain. Herculine/Alexina is not reveling in the sexual pleasures produced by his/her happy limbo of nonidentity; nor is he/she concerned with whether these pleasures are subversive or not. Herculine is in torment; his/her gender identity does not fit into the norm that his/her society prescribes. As a result he/she is deprived of the love and acceptance that all subjects seek, and, ultimately, also of life.

What would a therapist do with Herculine's pain? Clearly the limbo of nonidentity was not a happy one for him/her. Not to have a gender identity is not a happy option that produces a satisfying, healthy life. Herculine wanted an identity and the love that accompanies it, yet neither Foucault nor Butler seems willing to concede this. Nor can their theories offer any insight into how Herculine's pain could be relieved or how he/she could lead a satisfying life. On the contrary, they seem to want to use his/her pain as a vehicle for revealing and destabilizing gender norms.

Layton suggests that after *Gender Trouble*, Butler moves closer to object relations theory, a move Layton defines as "modernist." This conclusion is inaccurate. Butler is adamantly opposed to any conception of a core self, even the relational core that object relations theory proposes. For her object relations theory is essentialist and, hence, unacceptable. Layton herself confirms this in her discussion of the plight of a particular patient: "Sheila's longing to be consistent is a longing that nearly all postmodern theorists pathologize and condemn as inherently oppressive" (1998, 132). Butler is much too committed to this conception of the subject to abandon it for a theory that she regards as seriously compromised by modernism.

The force of the accounts of Glass and Layton lies in their real-world connection, the evidence they provide that outside the rarified atmosphere of postmodern theory this conception of the subject is not only untenable but painful. Marta Caminero-Santangelo provides another perspective on this problem in *The Madwoman Can't Speak: Or Why Insanity Is Not Subversive* (1998). Caminero-Santangelo attacks what she defines as a pervasive theme in feminist literary criticism: madness as a resistance strategy for women. Through a careful analysis of this genre of literature she makes the obvious point that madwomen are silenced. The asylum accounts that have become so popular in recent years rest on a fundamental paradox: to listen to *former* madwomen speak about their experiences is to recognize that madwomen, when they are mad, cannot themselves speak (43). Like Glass and Layton, Caminero-Santangelo argues that no agency is possible without a sense of oneself as an "I" (102). The splintered self of the madwoman can neither act nor resist. She concludes her account by arguing, "Instead of privileging the retreat into madness, then, let us privilege the forms of agency and of active creative transformation in all its forms, which women engage in" (181).

My thesis in the following is that the concept of the subject that best addresses the issues raised by contemporary discussions of identity is found, at least in outline form, in object relations theory. Object relations theory supplies a core subject, but it is a core that is, like that of the postmodern subject, constituted through discourse and relational experience. Object relations theory demonstrates that we can theorize a coherent subject without abandoning social construction. We need not, unlike Alcoff and, to a certain extent, Butler, retreat to the modernist subject to supply agency and coherency; social construction does not obviate coherency. Further, I will argue that the subject of object relations theory also avoids one of the major problems of the postmodern subject: monolithic cultural determinism. Butler has no way of explaining why some people conform to hegemonic norms while others refuse them. Object relations theory, by exploring the way in which subjects are constituted by their early relationships, can explain how subjects differ; it builds difference into the very formation of identity. Early relationships give subjects tools with which they negotiate their experiences in later life. Because those early experiences differ individually and culturally, the way subjects negotiate those experiences will also necessarily differ. The self posited by object relations theory is neither "true" nor fully determined by discourse but rather a continuously evolving negotiation between a relationally constructed self and the world that self encounters.

In the current climate of feminist discussions of identity, an argument for object relations theory needs considerable defense. Chodorow's *The Reproduction of Mothering* (1978) brought the theory to the forefront of feminist discussions. Gilligan's reliance on the theory in *In a Different Voice* (1982) had the effect of identifying it with the difference feminism of the 1980s. In the 1990s Jane Flax (1990), Christine Di Stefano (1991), and Nancy Hirschmann (1992) championed object relations theory as an alternative to postmodernism. Since then, however, the theory has fallen into disrepute. It has been dismissed as essentialist and homogenizing. Its critics argue that it assumes that women and only women mother and that this "mother" represents all women. It is alleged to be homogenizing in the sense that differences between mothers—race, class, ethnicity, and so on—are erased by the theory. Object relations theory, in sum, is interpreted as out of sync with the dominant theme of contemporary feminism: differences between women.

I will not deny certain aspects of these criticism in my assessment of object relations theory. My intent, however, is to present an interpretation of the theory that speaks to many of the issues raised in the current debate over identity and identity politics. My argument is that, far from denying difference, it is possible to use object relations theory to explain differences between women in a way that many other feminist theories cannot. Specifically, I argue that by exploring the details of identity formation in early childhood, object relations theory provides a means of explaining both cultural and individual influences in identity formation, giving an explanation that is lacking in the cultural determinism of many contemporary feminist theories.

The roots of object relations theory lie in developments in child psychology that had no connection to feminism. This in itself is significant. Feminists have used the theory to explain the development of gender identity. But the originators of object relations theory were attempting to explain the most basic element of identity: how human beings acquire a sense of self. These theorists were focused exclusively on the nuclear family in Western societies, in which women are the primary parent. Unfortunately, they did not specify that historical locatedness as much as they should have. It does not follow, however, that the theory is necessarily limited to this social and historical situation. It can be expanded beyond these narrow confines to accommodate a variety of social situations in a variety of historical eras.

At the heart of object relations theory is the claim, developed most notably by W. D. Winnicott, that the child, specifically the infant, does not have a given self that emerges as the child develops; rather, the self emerges and is constituted by the relationships it experiences. As Winnicott puts it, an infant is not a being, but a "going-on being" who is called into existence by the nurturing environment that the caretaker provides (1965, 57, 86). What is called into being in these relationships is what I will call the core self. It is important to note at the outset, however, that the core self is not a "true" or "essential" self as the modernists understood it but, rather, the product of relationships, a socially constituted entity. It is significant that Winnicott uses the language of illusion and symbolism to describe this concept of the self. Discussing the process of maturation, Winnicott states, "At a later stage the live body with its limits, and with an inside and outside, is *felt by the individual* to form the core of the imaginative self" (1975, 245–47). In his descriptions of the process by which the self develops, Winnicott makes no absolute distinctions between the illusory, symbolic, and "real" dimensions of experience.

The early object relations theorists were acutely aware of the fact that their approach to the self represented a radical departure in psychological theory. Many object relations theorists defined their position as a "paradigm shift" in psychology, the movement away from a given, essential, or true self to a relational, socially constituted self. One of the proponents of this shift, Steven Mitchell, appeals to Thomas Kuhn to argue that the shift from drive theory to relational theory in psychology is parallel to shifts in other fields toward a nonfoundational perspective (1988, 17). As with any generalization, there are exceptions to this statement. John Bowlby, one of the advocates of the theory, wants to retain a biological base by arguing that the child's attachment to the mother is a biological need (1988). But even Bowlby argues that the relational model, what he calls "attachment theory," represents a paradigm shift and, significantly, entails a new conception of science to accommodate it.

This is an aspect of object relations theory that is ignored by most contemporary feminist theorists. Like many feminists, object relations theorists define themselves nonfoundationally, as representing a shift away from the modernist paradigm of essences and absolutes. Furthermore, they argue that this shift necessarily entails a new approach to science, a scientific method that can accommodate relationships, meanings, and nuance. All this is consistent with the social constructionist approach I am advocating. It reinforces my argument for the relevance of object relations theory for contemporary discussions of identity.

Object relations theorists, furthermore, are very clear that their approach entails a conception of human nature radically at odds with that informing Freudian theory. Mitchell writes: "The evidence seems overwhelming that the infant does not *become* social through learning or conditioning, or through our adaptation to reality, but that the infant is programmed to be social. Relatedness is not a means to some other end (tension reduction, pleasure, or security); the very nature of the infant draws him into relationship" (1988, 24). In a statement reminiscent of Butler, Mitchell argues, "A personality is not something one has, but something one does." Consistent patterns develop, but these are not reflective of something inside; rather, they reflect learned modes of dealing with situations (25). But while Butler looks solely to cultural patterns to explain the emergence of personality/identity, the object relations theorists look deeper. They look underneath cultural influences in the development of these patterns to the individual character of the parents and, particularly, the mother. Since the child's character is formed through connection to the parent, it follows that the parents' particular social situation and unique personalities must be central to the formation of identity.

The significant contribution of object relations theory is that the theory combines attention to social, cultural construction with an analysis of the idiosyncratic nature of each individual human life. The basic tenet of object relations theory is that the self is created from meanings assigned to experience. Those meanings come from the social context into which the individual is born. But each individual will have different experiences that will be filtered through those social meanings. Understanding that life entails an appreciation of those circumstances and experiences. Our nature is social—"[e]mbeddedness is endemic to the human experience" (Mitchell 1988, 276). But I am social in interaction with *specific* others, and understanding identity must attend to both the general (social) and the specific (individual). In other words, we are all embedded but we are all embedded differently at different locations.[5]

Although the relational model developed by object relations theorists is

5. Jürgen Habermas (1992, 1979) also identifies a "paradigm shift" in the rejection of a pregiven subject. He looks to the work of George Herbert Mead to theorize this subject, specifically Mead's distinction between the "I" and the "me" (Mead 1959). But Mead, like many cultural determinists, is focused exclusively on cultural meanings and fails to explore the creation of individual identity beyond those meanings.

founded on the relationship of mother and child, the theorists of this model do not explore, or, for that matter, even mention the gender implications of the theory. But these implications are significant. As feminist theorists will argue, object relations theory constitutes a paradigm shift in another sense: a shift from a concept of self that privileges masculine qualities of autonomy and separation to one that defines these qualities as aberrant and privileges relationship, traditionally the realm of the feminine. The theorist who initially advances this theory is, of course, Nancy Chodorow. Chodorow's *The Reproduction of Mothering* (1978), although it adds little to object relations theory, describes the implications of the theory for gender identity and brought the theory to the attention of the feminist community.

Chodorow begins with the premise that women's appropriate gender role cannot be explained by explicit ideological instruction or formal coercion (1978, 33). The social reproduction of gender roles, she argues, is not a product of intention but, rather, is "embedded in and fundamental to the social organization of gender" (34). It is important to note that, from the outset, Chodorow grounds her theory in history. Women's mothering, she asserts, is not an unchanging transcultural universal; "woman's role as we know it is an historical product" (32). Many of the criticisms of Chodorow's work have centered on the ahistoricism and homogeneity of her theory. But it is clear from these passages that Chodorow sees the social reproduction of mothering as a particular historical occurrence rooted in particular social practices. Although we could argue that she does not mention this as often as she should, it is clear that historical embeddedness is integral to her approach. Furthermore, it is her conviction that the practices she describes are rooted in history that is the foundation of her belief that these practices can be changed.

The substance of Chodorow's theory—that the mother's different relationship with her daughter as opposed to that with her son produces sharply different gender identities—is well known. It forms the basis of Carol Gilligan's influential theory of the different moral voices of men and women. This aspect of object relations theory will not be the focus of my account. Instead I will concentrate on two aspects of Chodorow's theory that are relevant to my thesis. The first is her assertion that what she calls "unidirectional cultural determinism" is inadequate (1978, 47). Although Butler had not yet written her influential book, Chodorow's critique is particularly applicable to *Gender Trouble*. Cultural determinists argue that cultural values are directly transmitted to individuals. But they do not explore how that transmission takes place or the practices that affect that transmission. They do not explore the myriad influences on the child—cultural, social, familial, class—that together constitute the child's emerging identity. Unless we explore these factors, Chodorow argues, we cannot explain the emergence of gender identity.

I would add to this that unless we explore these factors, we cannot explain why we do not all turn out the same. If, as the cultural determinists argue, culture imprints us all, then why are we not all social dupes? Chodorow's answer is complex: "All aspects of psychic structure, character, and emotional and erotic life are socially constituted through a 'history of object choices.' This history, dependent on the individual personalities and behavior of those who happen to interact with the child is also socially patterned according to the family structure and prevalent psychological modes of a society" (1978, 50). In other words, we are all socially constructed and embedded, but that social construction is not monolithic. Rather, it is translated by the individual characters and situations of those who raise us and therefore varies in multiple ways. There is both pattern and difference. We are all socialized to be "woman" but the filter of that socialization differs in ways we need to explore.

What I am arguing here is that Chodorow's theory contains elements that do not so much contradict as complicate her well-known thesis. Yes, the general pattern is for girls to develop relational capabilities and boys to develop autonomy. But those patterns vary widely within each gender, and they vary by the factors Chodorow cites: family structure, class, ethnicity, the economy, the mother's relationship to the father, and the individual characters of the parents. If we look at these factors we can see both the general pattern and the variation within the pattern. Most important, the variations within the pattern can explain why some of us resist gender norms and others conform to them.

This point is very important for my assessment of the relevance of object relations theory to questions of identity. Despite the fact that object relations theory is dismissed as monocausal and ahistorical, a careful reading of the theory reveals that it is in fact exactly the opposite. Because object relations theory claims that identity is formed in early childhood relationships and because those relationships necessarily differ from child to child, it follows that the assessment of difference is built into the foundation of the theory. Using object relations theory demands that we look at how cultural values are transmitted through the individual situations of individual children. Feminists have used the theory to emphasize the difference that gender makes. But the theory encompasses more than gender. It demands that we look at the full range of differences that structure identity. In other words, far from being monocausal, object relations theory is rooted in difference.

The second factor of Chodorow's theory that I want to emphasize is her assertion that out of the relational experiences, a core self emerges. Chodorow argues that "[w]hat is internalized from an ongoing relationship becomes un-conscious and persists more or less independent of that original relationship. It may be generalized as a feeling of self-in-relationship and set up as a per-manent feature of psychic structure and the experience of self" (1978, 50). This is what Winnicott refers to as the "true" or central self. This "relatively stable foundation" is the basis upon which other forms of relational development will be built. It exerts what Chodorow refers to as a "powerful influence" in later life (164). It is the sense of self, in lay person's terms, that allows us to func-tion in the world, to feel that we have a particular identity that continues throughout our life. It is the sense of identity that is missing in the fragmented selves that Glass and Layton discuss.

This is the sense of self that I earlier referred to as the ungrounded ground. I agree with Glass, Layton, and Chodorow that the core self that these the-orists discuss is necessary for psychic health. We cannot live satisfying or even viable lives without this core self. But to make this argument does not entail positing an essential, pregiven self. It is a self that is socially constructed from the relational experiences of childhood, but it is nonetheless stable and ongoing. It is the basis from which we negotiate all the experiences we en-counter subsequent to its formation. It is an ungrounded ground but a ground nevertheless.

Chodorow does not mention postmodernism in *The Reproduction of Moth-ering* because it was not a major influence in feminism at the time she wrote the book. But when Jane Flax published *Thinking Fragments: Psychoanalysis, Feminism, and Postmodernism in the Contemporary West* in 1990, postmodernism was one of the major topics of her discussion. Her presentation of object re-lations theory thus is colored by its relation to postmodernism. One of the central theses of the book is that object relations theory and Winnicott in par-ticular offer an alternative to the fragmented subject of postmodernism on the one hand and the "natural" subject of modernism on the other. Like Lay-ton and Glass, Flax argues against the fragmented self of postmodernism be-cause it makes a satisfying life impossible. She asserts, "Persons who have a core self find the experience of those who lack or have lacked it almost unimag-inable" (1990, 219).

What is curious about Flax's position, however, is that in her subsequent work she seems to back down on her advocacy of a core self. In *Disputed Sub-jects: Essays on Psychoanalysis, Politics, and Philosophy* (1993) she writes, "People can achieve a coherency or long-term stability without claiming or construct-ing a (false or true) solid core self" (102–3). Now she describes subjectivity as "not all illusion," but a "shifting and always changing intersection of complex, contradictory, and unfinished processes" (108). It is difficult to explain this seeming repudiation of object relations theory. I think what we are seeing here is evidence of the move away from object relations theory that characterizes the post-*Gender Trouble* 1990s. Butler's repudiation of anything smacking of the modernist subject is so powerful that it drowns out other alternatives. Few feminist theorists in the 1990s advocate object relations theory as a viable position. At most some, like Alcoff, advocate a kind of hybrid position that incorporates modernist and postmodernist positions.[6] Object relations theory had a good run in the 1980s. Gilligan's immensely influential *In a Different Voice* was rooted in object relations theory. Feminist psychoanalysts found the position useful in both theory and practice (Jack 1991; Jordon 1991). But the criticisms of "difference feminism" ultimately defeated the position. Critics claimed that any position rooted in a monolithic category of "woman" erased differences between women and perpetuated hierarchy. Because object relations theory was closely associated with difference feminism it, too, was repudiated.

Chodorow's 1999 book, *The Power of Feeling: Personal Meaning in Psychoanalysis, Gender, and Culture*, speaks to this repudiation. Twenty-one years after her pathbreaking book, Chodorow is no longer articulating an up-and-coming theory but, rather, is defensive about a position that has fallen from favor. She is acutely aware that the theory she helped to establish is no longer acceptable to most feminists. The thesis of Chodorow's book is that personal psychodynamic meanings are constitutive of meaning in general and are as influential as culture, language, or discourse in this process. She asserts that personal meaning created by the power of feeling is central to human life and thus that subjectivity is equally shaped by inner and outer experiences (1999, 5). She further argues that the capacities that enable us to create personal meaning are innate human capacities that develop from birth in a context of interaction with others (14).

The object of Chodorow's attack is what she calls "essentialist culturalism," the assumption that all meaning is culturally created. Against this she argues for an "inner reality" that creates meaning along with culture. This inner reality on Chodorow's account is the capacity for transference, projection, introjection, and unconscious fantasy that creates the private language of the self. Her thesis is that throughout the individual's life this inner reality interacts with the outer reality of culture to form meanings. Although Chodorow claims that transference is already a social relationship, she still wants to maintain the distinction between inner and outer realities (14–26). Most important, she wants to define transference as universal, "one of the great abilities and defining capacities of the human mind" (21).

6. See my discussion in Hekman 1995.

Chodorow's conclusion is straightforward: cultural meaning does not precede individual meaning (76). Rather, "[f]rom earliest infancy, meaning is always tinged with projection, emotion, and fantasy and is not merely linguistic or cognitive" (64). Chodorow is also very clear about the theoretical implications of her position. She states: "With this psychoanalytic argument, I am making a universal claim about human subjectivity and its constituent psychodynamic processes, just as a cultural or poststructuralist theorist might universalize the equally essentialist claim that subjectivity is linguistically or discursively constituted" (76).

Gender is not the subject of *The Power of Feeling*. But Chodorow makes it clear that her position has direct relevance to the question of how gender identity is formed. She argues that each person's sense of gender fuses personal meaning that is created psychodynamically and idiosyncratically from within and cultural meanings from without (126). What we call our gender identity thus is a combination of these two sources of meaning. There is a significant advantage to this position. It allows Chodorow to simultaneously talk about patterns of gender socialization and individual gender identity (107). All women are socialized into the gender identity of "woman" that is hegemonic in our society. But that socialization is affected by particular others, most notably our family, who interpret the hegemonic concept in a particular way. The result is a specific gender identity that shares qualities with others in the category but is, ultimately, uniquely our own.

One way of characterizing Chodorow's thesis here is that she takes a "both/and" stance. She does not want to deny the cultural creation of meaning, but she cannot accept the position of what she calls essentialist culturalism that denies individuals an inner life. Chodorow's resolution makes an important contribution. She is right to assert that cultural determinism cannot explain why we do not all turn out the same. It cannot explain individual differences in the category "woman." Just as important, it cannot explain the existence of an inner life, the sense of personal identity that we all possess. Chodorow's both/and approach corrects this lacuna in cultural determinism. But Chodorow goes too far in the direction of the essentialist self in her attempt to articulate a theory of individual identity. She claims that every individual has the capacity to create intrapsychic meaning. This is an important and valid point. But then she separates this capacity from the linguistic, creating an opposition between the psychodynamic and the linguistic. It is not necessary to take this tack in order to claim the existence of an inner reality. Object relations theory has taught us that in infancy the child develops a sense of self, a core self, in relationship with others. The child must be born with the capacity to achieve this. But the process of achieving this self is thoroughly social. It need not entail acceptance of a prelinguistic psychodynamic realm.

Chodorow's goal in *The Power of Feeling* is laudable. We need a theory that can account for individual variations in the expression of cultural meanings. We need a theory that can explain individual identity and meaning creation. But that theory need not appeal to a prelinguistic realm of personal meaning. I would like to amend Chodorow's theory by arguing that each of us forms a core self through relational experiences in early childhood and this core self provides us with a stable, individual identity that carries us through life. It is the base from which we negotiate the experiences we encounter later in life. But this self, like the cultural experiences we negotiate, is also thoroughly social. As Chodorow argues, cultural meaning is always individually communicated (1999, 215). But the individual who does this communicating is also socially constituted.

One of the advantages of the perspective I am advocating is that it can explain how individuals negotiate their experiences in later life and why they negotiate them differently. At the center of object relations theory is the claim that each of us acquires a core self in childhood that is the product not only of cultural influences, but also of family structure, class, ethnicity, and the individual characteristics of those with whom we interact. As a result, although there will be overall patterns in gender identity, there will also be differences. Each individual's gender identity is a product not only of overall cultural patterns but also of his/her unique situation and experiences. It follows from this that as individual women negotiate the experiences of adolescence and adulthood, and, particularly, as they encounter the hegemonic ideal of "woman" in our culture, their reactions will not be identical. Some will conform to that ideal, some will resist it, and some will, as the postmoderns argue, find the interstices between hegemonic concepts and exploit the slippage that results. What is significant, however, is that the cultural determinists cannot explain where those differences originate; object relations theory can.[7]

The cases discussed in a recent collection, *Reinventing Identities: The Gendered Self in Discourse* (Bucholtz, Liang, and Sutton 1999), illustrates the points I am trying to make here. The volume begins with the assumption that the problem of contemporary feminism is the problem of identity. The authors

7. In *Thinking Fragments*, Flax argued: "An adequate theory of human development from an object relations perspective would have to include an account of all these different levels [parents, social structure, etc.] and types of social relations and their interactions, mutual determinations and possible antagonisms" (1990, 124). My argument here has been that object relations theory can supply such a theory.

examine how different groups of girls and women negotiate the hegemonic concept of "woman." They discuss how deviant identities use hegemonic discourse to make their identities coherent. They discuss how girls negotiate puberty and how these negotiations differ across class and race. They discuss how aspects of that hegemonic concept can quite literally drive a particular woman to madness (Capps 1999). The conclusion I want to draw from these examples is that the negotiations of identity these authors describe would make no sense without assuming that each of the individual girls/women discussed possessed a core identity from which these negotiations emanated. One cannot negotiate from a void. There must be a ground—I would argue an ungrounded ground but a ground nonetheless—from which the individual assesses and reacts to experience.

These descriptions would also not make sense unless we can assume that individual women's core selves differ in significant ways. Several articles illustrate that Hispanic girls negotiate their experiences in school based on the pattern of socialization they experienced at home, a pattern different from that of Anglo girls. The thesis of the article describing the woman driven to agoraphobia was that she was influenced by elements of her socialization that made her susceptible to this condition. Other women might have avoided it even under the same circumstances. My point is that unless we make these assumptions explicit we cannot understand gender identity. It is not necessary to choose between similarity—a common identity for woman—or differences. It is not necessary to choose between a culturally determined subject and the autonomous essentialist subject. Rather, we can embrace a theory that explains both patterns and differences, that examines the power of the hegemonic concept of "woman" and the different ways in which that concept is transmitted to individuals. It can explain how individuals acquire a coherent, core self from which they make choices and negotiate experiences without assuming an essentialist pregiven self.

One of the most influential arguments against the difference feminism with which object relations theory has been associated is put forth in Elizabeth Spelman's *Inessential Woman* (1988). Spelman's persuasive argument that the concept of "woman" is inherently hierarchical and erases differences between women was decisive in the turn toward differences and away from difference. In the course of her book Spelman criticizes Chodorow's theory on the grounds that it ignores influences other than gender in the formation of identity. But Spelman also notes that Chodorow's account points to a more complicated understanding of gender than she herself develops (82). This account was never pursued, however, because object relations theory became synonymous with the difference feminism that was rejected in the 1990s.

This rejection is unwarranted. A careful application of object relations theory to the question of gender identity has significant advantages for feminist theory. It can explain the different ways in which hegemonic gender identity is transmitted to individuals. It can incorporate, and indeed demands, the incorporation of differences of race, class, and other factors into the understanding of the construction of each individual's gender identity. It can incorporate both general patterns and individual differences. And, most important, it can explain the evolution of a coherent, core self without retreating to essentialism.

These advantages are most clearly evident in an analysis of adolescent girls co-authored by Carol Gilligan (Taylor, Gilligan, and Sullivan 1995). The authors of *Between Voice and Silence: Women and Girls, Race and Relationship* (hereafter *BVS*) examine the experiences of a racially mixed group of twenty-six girls from a poor and working-class school as they negotiate the transition to adolescence. All the girls in the study had been defined as "at risk" of leaving school, becoming pregnant, or both. This study is a continuation of two earlier studies in which Gilligan and her colleagues had examined the vulnerability of girls at the crucial juncture of adolescence and, especially, the role played by their relationships to adult women in this period (Gilligan, Lyons, and Hanmer 1990; Brown and Gilligan 1992). These previous studies made a significant contribution to the understanding of the development of girls and the role played by adult women in this development. But they were also liable to criticism. Because they were conducted on girls from white, privileged backgrounds, the studies fueled the criticism of Gilligan's approach as incapable of accommodating differences between women. To its critics these studies proved that Gilligan's approach in particular and object relations theory in general are not only incapable of dealing with differences between women but also foster the hierarchical concept of "woman" that was the object of Spelman's critique.[8]

The work of Gilligan and her co-authors in *BVS* reveals the errors of these critiques. What emerges from this study is that Gilligan's approach, and, I would argue, object relations theory more generally, provides a method that constitutes a major advance in the analysis of identity formation. Gilligan and her colleagues approach the question of identity from three interrelated directions. First, the authors look for overall patterns. Through their in-depth interviews with the girls, they discern certain similarities in the issues the girls face at this significant period of their lives. These similarities provide the start-

8. It is significant that there were black women in the group of women that Gilligan studied for *In a Different Voice* but Gilligan did not identity them as such (Marcus et al. 1995, 208). At this point racial differences between women were not the focus of Gilligan's study; later they became central.

ing point for the questions the interviewers ask. The second direction of analysis is the examination of differences. In a highly nuanced analysis, the authors argue that what they call the girls' different social and cultural locations produce different ways in which the overall patterns are experienced. Race in particular plays a major role in constituting these differences. The third direction is power. Although this line of analysis is less developed than the other two, it nevertheless plays a significant background role. The power of what cultural determinists call the hegemonic concept of woman is very present to these girls, influencing the choices they make in their particular social locations.

Gilligan is famous for her patterns. She first established her reputation arguing that women's pattern of moral reasoning is different from that of men. What is significant about *BVS* is that the patterns this study reveals are the same patterns revealed in the study of the privileged white girls. The thesis of the book is the same as that of the two previous studies: at adolescence, girls risk losing touch with what they know through experience. Their sense of themselves is at odds with images of the good or desirable woman (Taylor, Gilligan, and Sullivan 1995, 4). At adolescence a shift takes place for many girls as they experience a relational impasse and a developmental crisis. As the authors put it. "To be in relationship at this juncture jeopardizes 'relationship'" (23). As they enter adolescence the simple truths of their relationships with others come into conflict with what is expected of them as "selfless" women. Gilligan's thesis is that this conflict is a societal pattern that affects all women, the "chill wind of tradition" that defines women's place in our culture (Gilligan, Lyons, and Hanmer 1990, 20).

Another pattern that emerges is that all the girls grapple with the problem of learning to speak—about what and to whom. Mother-daughter relationships are crucial to this learning. Mothers teach daughters to "fit in," but "revisit their own development and face their own relationship to culture in an intensely personal and often conflictual way" (Taylor, Gilligan, and Sullivan 1995, 70). Girls speak to their mothers but also learn how and whether to speak to others: "Learning what subjects are appropriate to speak about, as well as to whom it is appropriate to speak and who is trustworthy, is part of adolescent development—part of girls' initiation into womanhood" (75). As they move into adolescence, girls frequently have to renegotiate their relationships with their mothers, often becoming less open, particularly about sex.

The final pattern the authors discuss concerns adult women's relationship to girls. In interview after interview the girls reveal that they feel let down by adult women, not only their mothers, but also other women with whom they have a relationship. The authors go so far as to call this a "betrayal," a failure to support girls when they most need support (143). The study concludes that it is in the eighth grade that girls most need this support, most need the intervention of adult women to help them over this difficult period. But it also concludes that this is when they do not receive this support.

These patterns are significant. They provide the overall structure of the girls' experiences. But for the purposes of my thesis, the most important aspect of the analysis in *BVS* is that for each of the patterns the researchers uncovered they found corresponding differences as well. Each pattern is negotiated differently because of differences in class, race, culture, or the individual situations of the girls. Furthermore, the study demonstrates that there is no conflict in talking simultaneously about patterns and differences. Rather, it illustrates how the analysis of patterns and differences form an analytic unity. That significant changes occur as girls move into adolescence seems obvious. That this experience will be constituted by culture, race, and class seems equally obvious. As the interviews proceeded, the distinctions between these two directions of analysis blurred.

The students who were interviewed were first asked to identity themselves in terms of race/ethnicity. Although the students did so, the researchers noted that these categories were themselves too broad, erasing differences, for example, differences of class, within them (20). But this initial question revealed one of the most fundamental differences noted by the researchers: a cultural difference in the sense of "I." The African worldview embodies an extended concept of "I" beyond the self. Hispanics place the welfare of the family/community above that of the individual. These cultural differences affected how the students identified themselves as individuals.

In order to explain those differences, the researchers developed the concept of "secondary cultural differences": characteristics that are not a part of primary culture, but develop in the context of racism (49). For example, they noted that the socialization of African American girls is less stereotypical than that of white middle- and upper-middle-class girls. For black girls there is less emphasis on cultivating the qualities of idealized femininity, more on strength and self-sufficiency (43). Differences also emerged around the issues of speaking and silence. Hispanic girls frequently silence themselves in this crucial developmental period. Hispanic culture teaches girls to be respectful, conforming, dependent, obedient, virtuous, and loyal to family. It also teaches them not to talk about boys and sex (60).

The researchers discovered other particular cultural differences in the relationships between girls and their mothers. With regard to one of the girls, the researchers note: "Diane's experience of her relationship with her mother, like all relationships, occurs in a particular context of race and social class, one in which women have traditionally held multiple roles as economic providers, mothers, wives, lovers, community and church organizers and workers" (76). In another case they note that Sandy's "logic" when she discusses her relationship with her mother and her reasons for wanting a baby are informed by "culture, social class, and her particular family situation" (111–12). For black and Hispanic girls there are cultural traditions that can ease the tension with their mothers: the "othermother" tradition in black communities and the "comadres" tradition in Hispanic and Portuguese communities (117). The researchers conclude: "Issues of trust and intimacy, central to any process of group formation, immediately become more complicated and layered in the presence of different cultural norms about the extent to which it is appropriate or safe to express strong feelings and share personal information" (159). But unless these cultural differences are expressed, they assert, the girls' separation by race, class, and ethnicity cannot be broken.

I could cite more examples of "secondary cultural differences" that are noted by the researchers, but the point of the analysis should be clear. All the girls in the study face the same developmental experience: the onset of adolescence and the concomitant necessity of confronting the hegemonic concept "woman." But the way in which they navigate that experience is influenced not only by broad cultural factors, but also by their particular location in the cultural matrix. To say that we are culturally located is to say that we are located in a particular place in culture. Thus to talk about our constitution by culture necessitates discussion of our differences. The two are not antithetical but, rather, logically linked.

The third direction of analysis in *BVS* is power, the hegemonic power of concepts and cultural practices that shape the girls' lives. This theme is closely connected to the first theme of cultural patterns. This is to be expected. The overall cultural patterns that structure the girls' development are experienced in terms of power; they exert a hegemonic force. This force must be negotiated if the girls are to successfully enter into womanhood. From the outset it was evident to the researchers that, despite their specific locations, the root of all the girls' problems was the fact that their sense of themselves was at odds with images of the good or desirable woman that pervades our culture (4). This is the hegemonic concept of "woman" that the cultural determinists theorize. The researchers note that the girls are under pressure from within and without to shape themselves in accordance with this dominant cultural ideal of femininity and womanhood (23).

Further, the issues of class, race, and ethnicity that structure the girls' perceptions are themselves issues of power. In a society structured by class and race, the girls' development is necessarily influenced by their status in that society. "Power differences constitute the social reality in which psychological development occurs" (29). The girls' perception of themselves as other, as excluded from the mainstream of society, affects them as they move into adolescence. They are seeking to conform to societal norms such as that of "Superwoman" while at the same time knowing that they have less chance of doing so than white middle-class girls. The otherness, furthermore, is perceived as a fact over which they have no control.

Although *BVS* speaks directly to the key issues affecting identity and identity formation, few references are made to the book in the contemporary feminist literature on identity. The exception to this is Cressida Heyes's analysis in *Line Drawings: Defining Women Through Feminist Practice* (2000). Heyes presents a favorable analysis of *BVS*, holding it up as an example of the kind of feminist method we should employ. Despite this praise, however, Heyes's book also represents precisely the attitude to object relations theory that I am trying to refute. The context of Heyes's argument is her assertion that the essentialist-constructionist dichotomy has outlived its usefulness in feminist theory. Her book is an attempt to displace this dichotomy and find another way to approach feminist theory and practice. Her first point is that *BVS* represents a departure from Gilligan's "essentialist" position. She then goes on to assert that the theoretical model of *BVS* is "increasingly tenuously" derived from object relations theory. To offer evidence of this, she argues that Gilligan supplements object relations theory with a theory of complex social ontology that conceptualizes healthy human lives as webs of relationship (Heyes 2000, 114).

It should be obvious that Heyes's perspective differs significantly from the one presented above. Despite this, however, the conclusions Heyes derives from her analysis of *BVS* are very similar to mine. Heyes argues that Gilligan's "rich and evocative" portrayal of adolescent girls is an invaluable contribution to feminist practice. The imperative facing antiessentialist feminists, she asserts, is not *whether* to make generalizations but how to make them (119–20). Although Heyes finds Gilligan's approach "undertheorized," she nonetheless applauds Gilligan's attempt to find both patterns and difference in adolescent girls' lives (128). In short, she finds Gilligan's analysis to be precisely what she is looking for: a feminist method that is antiessentialist yet makes carefully circumscribed generalizations.

Heyes's tentative and somewhat defensive advocacy of Gilligan is indicative of the feminist community's dismissive attitude to object relations theory in general and Gilligan in particular. The point of the foregoing has been to demonstrate that object relations theory, particularly in its feminist version, has never been essentialist but, rather, is "essentially" concerned with difference. The goal of my analysis of *BVS* was to highlight these advantages. The interrelated investigation of pattern, differences, and power that structures the book provides a complex and nuanced understanding of how identity functions in society. This analysis also reveals that the researchers' assumption of a core self, an ungrounded ground, is central to this understanding of identity and makes possible the negotiations of difference that define personal identity.

Heyes's tentative turn to Gilligan, despite Gilligan's low status in feminist circles, is also indicative in another sense: it is evidence of a growing discontent with the postmodern subject in feminist theory, a suspicion that a subject determined solely by cultural forces is inadequate. This discontent has turned other feminists in different directions. McNay (2000) looks to a narrative conception of self theorized by Ricoeur and Castoriadis. Benhabib (1999) also theorizes a narrative self. Weeks (1998) looks to a standpoint theory of subjectivity. Young counters the determinism of the postmodern subject with a simple claim: "Individuals are agents" (2000, 101) without explaining how this is possible.

In Chapter 3, I will expand the theory I have presented here to develop an understanding of the relationship between personal and public identities. My claim here is that object relations theory in its feminist interpretation solves many of the problems posed by feminist discussions of identity. In *Inessential Woman* Spelman states, "All women are women but there is no being who is only a woman" (1988, 102). The interpretation of object relations theory presented here offers a way to understand how one can be both a woman in the general sense and a particular woman who acts in the world and makes choices that are both circumscribed by the concept "woman" and particular to each woman's specific translation of that concept. It can also explain how the power of hegemonic concepts such as "woman" structure but do not completely determine personal identity. Finally, this position can explain why some women resist the hegemonic concept while others conform to it. Resistance is a phenomenon that flows from the different ways in which the hegemonic concept is translated to specifically located individuals. The postmoderns can only explain resistance from the top down, as a product of the instability of gender categories. The position presented here theorizes resistance from the bottom up, as a product of differences constituted by individuals' different social locations.

2

Identity and the Liberal Polity

Carole Pateman and the Liberal Individual

It has become a commonplace of intellectual commentators that the twentieth century has witnessed a paradigm shift in conceptions of knowledge and the self, a move away from modernism in all its guises. Universalism, absolutism, and abstraction are being displaced by localism, particularism, and situated knowledge. Central to this paradigm shift is the rejection of the modernist subject, the pregiven, rational, autonomous self that is the linchpin of modernist thought. Object relations theory has played a key role in this rejection. The relational, situated subject of object relations theory displaces the absolutism of the modernist subject and all that is entailed by it. This relational subject, furthermore, has been a key element in contemporary feminist thought. Like Gilligan, many feminists have defined the modernist subject as inherently masculine and moved to define a feminine, relational self as its counterpoint.[1]

The contemporary turn away from the modernist self and

1. See my *Moral Voices/Moral Selves* (1995) for an extended discussion of these issues.

toward a relational, particularized self, however, has not been universal. The roots of the modernist subject are deep. It pervades our philosophical conceptions, our moral theory, and our political institutions and practices. I am concerned here with one of the remaining bastions of the modernist subject in contemporary theory and practice: the neutral citizen of the liberal polity. My thesis is that the configuration of the neutral, abstract citizen of liberalism creates problems not only for women in the liberal polity but for all "others" who do not conform to the veiled identity of this citizen. To begin the story I want to tell about this citizen, I will look at Charles Taylor's ambitious attempt to trace the roots of the modernist subject. In *Sources of the Self: The Making of the Modern Identity* (1989) Taylor's goal is to examine the evolution of the modern sense of self and identity and its centrality to contemporary philosophical thought. At the heart of his argument is his assertion that this conception is a historical product, the result of particular historical situations. The picture that emerges from his analysis is one that is all too familiar. His thesis is that this individual is a "disengaged self, capable of objectifying not only the surrounding world but also his own emotions and inclinations, fears, and compulsions, achieving thereby a kind of distance and self-possession that allows him to act 'rationally'" (21).

Taylor credits Descartes with articulating the idea of disengagement, an idea that was "one of the most important developments in the modern era" (159). Another major contributor was Locke, "the greatest teacher of Enlightenment" because he brought together an account of the new science as valid knowledge intertwined with a theory of the rational control of the self. The result was the "ideal of rational responsibility" that forms the core of the modern subject (174).

But this is not all there is to this subject. Taylor traces a second major aspect of modern identity: "inner depths." In the late eighteenth century the modern subject came to be defined not solely by rational control but also by a new power: expressive self-articulation. This intensifies the sense of inwardness that, Taylor claims, originated in the thought of Saint Augustine. But on Taylor's account, this movement was problematic. It created a tension within the subject between a rationality that demands a disengagement with feelings and the demand to express those feelings (390).

I would like to draw a number of conclusions from Taylor's examination of the self that are relevant to my concerns. First, one of the themes of Taylor's analysis is the pervasiveness and persistence of the modern concept of the self. He quotes Iris Murdoch on the picture of the human agent that dominates modern moral philosophy: "[T]his man is with us still, free, independent, lonely, powerful, rational, responsible, brave, the hero of so many novels and books of moral philosophy" (Murdoch 1970, 80). Taylor himself concludes his study by asserting:

> [W]hat I hope emerges from this lengthy account of the growth of the modern identity is how all pervasive it is, how much it envelops us, and how deeply we are implicated in it: in a sense of self defined by the powers of disengaged reason as well as of the creative imagination, in the characteristically modern understandings of freedom and dignity and rights, in the ideals of self-fulfillment and expression, and in the demands of universal benevolence and justice. (1989, 503).

My second conclusion regards what Taylor refers to as the tension in the modern subject between the rational autonomous self and the self-reflexive inner self, the self of feelings and emotions. Locke, that "greatest teacher of Enlightenment," installed one aspect of the modern subject, the rational, abstract self, into the liberal polity as the abstract universal citizen. This public man embodies all the qualities of this aspect of the subject: rationality, autonomy, separation. The other aspect of the subject is not denied, but is relegated to the private, nonpolitical sphere. Central to the conception of liberalism that Locke articulates is the separation of the abstract citizen from the private individual with feelings, connections to others, and even love. These elements of the self, Locke firmly believes, have no place in the public, political sphere. Private differences between individuals are politically irrelevant.

Despite the breadth of his analysis, Taylor does not comment on the significance of this split for women and, most important, for the role of women in the political sphere. No mention is made of women, gender, or feminism until two pages before the end of the book. There, in a discussion of writers influenced by Nietzsche who explore how "high ethical and spiritual ideals are often interwoven with exclusions and relations of domination" Taylor notes: "And contemporary feminist critique has also contributed greatly to this understanding in showing how certain conceptions of the life of the spirit exclude women, according them a lesser place, or assume their subordination" (1989, 518–19).

I want to pick up this strand in Taylor's analysis of the subject and examine how the political version of the modern conception of the subject excludes women not just from the "life of the spirit" but from politics as well. But I also want to go beyond this exclusion to examine the effect of liberalism's abstract citizen on the status of identity in the liberal polity. My thesis will be that relegating feelings, emotions, and connections to the private sphere not only excludes women, who, since the beginning of Western thought, have represented this sphere, but also rules as illegitimate *any* particular identities in the political sphere. The variant of the modernist subject installed in liberalism dictates that universal citizens are all the same; they have no identity per se. We are equal before the law; justice is blind. The particularities of our identities belong in the private, not the public, sphere.

In order to substantiate this thesis, I will rely on the feminist critique of the liberal individual developed by Carole Pateman. The feminist critique of the liberal/modernist individual is by no means the only critique that has been developed in the twentieth century. Indeed, critiques of this subject proliferated in twentieth-century thought. Nor is Pateman's critique unique in the feminist literature. Nancy Hartsock (1983), Susan Moller Okin (1989), Nancy Hirschmann (1992), and Christine Di Stefano (1991), among others, have offered cogent critiques of the liberal individual from a feminist perspective. All these authors argue that the masculinity of this individual relegates women to an inferior status in the liberal polity. These critiques are important and insightful. Together they establish a compelling feminist analysis of the problem of the liberal citizen. I am focusing here on Pateman's analysis, however, for a very particular reason: her approach offers the clearest connection to the problems raised by identity politics. The specific configuration of Pateman's analysis facilitates the goal of my examination: putting the phenomenon of identity politics in a new light. The critique of the liberal individual expressed by Pateman reveals why this practice is so problematic in the liberal polity.

The story that Pateman develops in her pathbreaking book, *The Sexual Contract* (1988), is a story about contracts. Contracts are the constitutive force of liberal society; they create the political basis of that society and sustain it through myriad contractual relationships. Despite the centrality of contracts for liberal society, however, not everyone is capable of entering into these relationships. At the heart of liberal theory is the assumption that "[o]nly masculine beings are endowed with the attributes and capacities necessary to enter into contracts, the most important of which is ownership of property in the person; only men, that is to say, are individuals" (6). It follows that sexual difference is political difference. To be masculine is to have rationality and thus ownership of one's person; to be female is to have neither. To be masculine is to be a full member of society, both economically and politically. To be female is not to be either.

Pateman's analysis is most forceful when she focuses on the founders of classical liberalism. Locke in particular is clear about excluding women from the social contract. For Locke modern civil society is a brotherhood of men, a fraternal pact (77). It is in her analysis of Locke, furthermore, that Pateman develops the most controversial aspect of her thesis. Pateman asserts that social contract theorists smuggle social characteristics into the natural condition, most notably, sexual relations (41). Her thesis is that a *sexual* contract necessarily precedes the social contract that constitutes liberal society (110). The individual living in the state of nature who signs the social contract must have already signed a sexual contract, that is, must have subordinated a woman as wife and mother; he must be, in other words, head of household. The subordinated woman, furthermore, is excluded from the social contract by definition. She cannot be the head of household, the husband and father who signs the social contract.

Analyses of other theorists easily substantiate this thesis. Rousseau and even Freud argue that women are incapable of transcending their passions and hence incapable of the abstraction necessary for participation in the public sphere (102). Other theorists follow suit: Kant argues that women have no civil personality (169); the universalism of Hegel's civil society is restricted to men (178). But Pateman wants to do much more than offer a historical analysis. She wants to argue that liberalism today excludes women from the public sphere because women continue to be excluded from the liberal definition of "individual." This definition did not become obsolete when women were granted the franchise.

Key to Pateman's argument in defense of this thesis is her analysis of John Rawls's *A Theory of Justice* (1971). The parties in Rawls's original position are defined as sexless but also, tellingly, as heads of families (Pateman 1988, 43). It would be easy to conclude from this that the most influential contemporary theorist of liberalism continues the tradition of defining the individual as masculine and presupposing a previous sexual contract. This is not an illegitimate conclusion, but it is not the center of Pateman's argument. Rather, she advances an epistemological argument about the relationship between public and private that informs liberalism. Women are the opposite of the civil law. They represent what man must master to bring civil society into being (102). Thus "[t]he civil sphere gains its universal meaning in opposition to the private sphere of natural subjection and womanly capacities" (113). Most pointedly, "[t]he civil individual and the public realm appear universal only in relation to and in opposition to the private sphere, the natural foundation of civil life. Similarly, the meaning of civil liberty and equality, secured and distributed impartially to all 'individuals' through the civil law, can be understood only in opposition to natural subjection (of women) in the private sphere" (114).

Another way of putting this is that liberty and equality are the attributes of the fraternity that exercises what Pateman calls "the law of male sex right" (1988, 114). As Pateman sees it, there is a double conjuring trick going on here. The sexual contract is hidden in the "natural" sphere and thus not examined or brought into the public sphere. But in addition, the fraternity that constitutes the public sphere is defined as universal. As Pateman puts it, "What better notion to conjure with than 'fraternity' and what better conjuring trick than to insist that 'fraternity' is universal and nothing more than a metaphor for community" (114). The result of these conjuring tricks is that both the false universality of the citizen of the liberal polity and his preceding sexual contract are hidden from public view.

The opposition between the public and the private dictates another characteristic of the public sphere that Pateman does not mention but that is nevertheless fundamental to the exclusions it creates. Liberalism defines not only the kind of entities that inhabit the public sphere but also the kind of discourse they can employ in that sphere. The antithesis between the public and the private entails that the individuals who inhabit the public sphere employ a certain kind of discourse that is distinctive to that sphere: a discourse of abstraction, rationality, and universality. This discourse is defined in opposition to that of the private sphere, which is particular and contextual. Political discourse is defined in terms of the abstraction that defines the citizen, the discourse of the private sphere in terms of the concrete and the specific.

In her book *In a Different Voice* (1982) Carol Gilligan has much to say about the gender implications of this distinction. Gilligan argues that men and women employ different moral voices, the justice voice and the care voice, respectively. She asserts that these voices are the product of the different childhood experiences of boys and girls. Boys develop rationality and autonomy because their mothers treat them as "little men" and encourage activities that foster these qualities. Girls develop nurturing and relational skills because their mothers attempt to reproduce themselves as mothers in their daughters. What is significant about this pattern is that the justice voice embodying masculine characteristics has been defined as the only true moral voice, what morality "really is." The care voice of women, in contrast, has been relegated to an inferior moral status, or, worse, defined as not truly moral.

This is not the place to elaborate on or defend Gilligan's thesis.[2] But I do want to connect the perspectives of Pateman and Gilligan. Gilligan's justice voice, the voice of the rational autonomous male, is the voice of the public sphere. Only arguments that are defined as "rational" in terms of this voice are deemed legitimate in political discourse. References to the particular and relational, Gilligan's care voice, are excluded. Furthermore, defining this voice as an inferior moral voice has significant political implications. True morality

2. See my *Moral Voices/Moral Selves* (1995).

is defined as the abstract universality that is necessary for discussions in the public sphere. Women's inability to employ the justice voice, their inability to abstract from the particular and concrete and ascend to the realm of abstract universal principles, excludes them from the public sphere. This exclusion, although central to liberalism, has deeper roots. Throughout the history of Western thought, women have been told that their inferior moral voice is insufficient to the demands of the public sphere.

Pateman brings together the elements of her argument to assert what should now be obvious: the construction of civil society defined by liberalism puts women in an impossible position. On the one hand a man's (citizen's) wife can be neither an "individual" nor a "citizen" (Pateman 1988, 179). Pateman's conclusion here is both sweeping and unequivocal: "The conclusion is easy to draw that the denial of civil equality to women means the feminist aspiration must be to win acknowledgment for women as 'individuals.' Such an aspiration can never be fulfilled. The 'individual' is a patriarchal category" (184). Women can never be full members of the liberal polity. Liberal feminism is an oxymoron. On the other hand, however, women are also doomed to try to achieve this equality. When contract and the individual hold sway, Pateman argues, women are left with no alternative but to try to become replicas of men (187). But women are incorporated into civil society on a different basis from that of men. The private sphere of women is separated from civil society. It both is and is not a part of it. Thus women both are and are not a part of the civil order (181). Their status is inherently ambiguous.

Underlying Pateman's argument here, as well as her prescription for what we might do about the problem she defines, is a fundamental assumption: there is no "neutral" human individual. In her critique of liberal theorists' attempts to define such an individual, she comments: "The attempt to set out the purely natural attributes of individuals is inevitably doomed to fail; all that is left if the attempt is consistent enough is a merely psychological biological or reasoning entity, not a human being" (41). Even Rawls's original position, she argues, is a logical construction; there is nothing human in it (43). If this is the case, then there is only one option for women: to enter civil society as *embodied* individuals: "Women can attain the formal standing of civil individuals but as embodied female beings we can never be 'individuals' in the same sense as men. To take embodied identity seriously demands the abandonment of the masculine, unitary individual to open up space for two figures: one masculine, one feminine" (224).

Although Pateman does not refer to object relations theory to make this argument, she, like the object relations theorists, theorizes a subject that constitutes a definitive rejection of the modernist subject. Like the object relations theorists, she proposes a subject that is situated and relational, that possesses particular rather than universal characteristics, a subject that is embodied, not abstract. But she adds an important dimension to this subject by placing it politically. She makes it clear that if we embrace the embodied subject everything, in a political sense, must change.

Unfortunately Pateman offers only the briefest outline of what this transformation entails. She identifies only two embodied citizens, one masculine, one feminine. But this is only the beginning of what is implied by allowing embodiment into citizenship. Gender is not the only form of embodiment or identity. Race, class, ethnicity, and many other factors come into play as well. At the end of the book Pateman seems to concede this by arguing that what she calls new social movements (presumably identity politics) raise issues similar to those raised by feminism but from a different perspective (223). In another context Pateman elaborates on this theme by arguing that feminists are trying to develop the first truly general theory in the Western world, one that includes women as well as men. She claims that feminism looks forward to a differentiated social order that includes both men and women as biologically differentiated but not unequal creatures (1989, 135–36). Furthermore, she has no illusions about how radical such a change would be. The theoretical and social transformation that is required if women and men are to be free and equal members of a democratic society, she argues, is as far reaching as can be imagined (52).

Pateman's critique of the liberal individual is profound; it cuts to the heart of the liberal polity, altering our conception of the functioning of that polity.[3] Although Pateman does not explicitly endorse object relations theory in her analysis, many of the assumptions of that theory are implicit in her approach. Other feminist critiques of liberalism, however, are specifically rooted in object relations theory. Christine Di Stefano uses object relations theory to claim that "[t]here is good reason to suppose that a specifically masculine cognitive orientation inhabits the terrain of modern political theory and enjoys a wide-ranging, if obscure and implicit, influence which has been underinterpreted to date (1991, 55). Nancy Hirschmann, although concerned specifically with the concept of obligation, employs object relations theory to develop an indictment of liberalism as a whole: "So object relations can be a means to understand how the problems of liberal democratic theory go beyond the empirical expulsion of women from politics to the fact that the epistemology from which these theories operate is premised as that exclusion" (1992, 169). She concludes,

---

3. For a compatible critique, see Dietz 1992.

like Pateman, that the social contract *requires* the exclusion of women from the political sphere (190).[4]

Feminist political theorists are not the only scholars concerned with the question of women and citizenship. Feminist historians have offered historical evidence in support of these critiques. In her analysis of the history of marriage in the United States, Nancy Cott (2000) argues that the marriage relationship, the subordination of the wife to the husband as head of the family, has been a pillar of U.S. politics and law since the eighteenth century. Legal marriage, Cott argues, has conferred a privileged status at the center of U.S. politics and society. The notion that the foundation of political society is the establishment of the husband as the head of household appears repeatedly throughout U.S. history. The argument that even propertyless men were able to govern their families was used to argue for manhood suffrage in the nineteenth century.[5] It also informed congressional policy for the Indians. Each Indian man's having a home of his own was declared "the way to start a people in the direction of civilization" (2000, 122).

Cott argues that recent court decisions have had the effect of "displacing marriage from the seat of official morality" (199). She describes this process as one of "disestablishment": "[O]ne could argue that the particular model of marriage which was for so long the officially supported one has been disestablished" (212). But Cott then goes on to cite several exceptions to this disestablishment and concludes, "Legal marriage remains a privileged public status, buttressed by government policies that allow and inspire people to have confidence in it" (224). Cott writes that the sexual contract is the "ballast for the form of government" (213) that we have known in the United States. The difficulty of removing that ballast serves to prove its centrality.

Linda Kerber takes a different tack in her analysis of women and citizenship in the United States (1998). Kerber argues that women have been classified as second-class citizens in the United States not because they have been excluded from the privileges of citizenship but because they have been denied citizenship's obligations. Beginning with an analysis of women's relationship to the state in the Revolutionary War, Kerber paints a picture in which women's obligation to their husbands overrides their obligation to the state. Thus women have been excused from accusations of treason and vagrancy; they have also been excused from jury service and, most notably, military service. Although,

4. Shane Phelan (2001) wants to take Pateman's critique beyond liberalism to include civic republicanism, which, she claims, still influences American conceptions of citizenship. For Phelan, lesbians, gay men, and bisexual and transgendered people in the United States are "sexual strangers," not citizens under this wider conception.

5. See also Brennan and Pateman 1979.

like Cott, Kerber argues that from 1971 on the legal status of women has changed radically, she also asserts that the legacy of coverture has not entirely disappeared from our political institutions.

The exclusion of women from the liberal polity is of overriding significance. The feminist critiques of the liberal individual as well as the historical evidence offered by feminist historians strongly establish this thesis. What I would like to argue, however, is that the significance of this thesis is not limited to the role of women in the liberal polity. It is my contention that this analysis has important significance not only for the role of women in liberalism but also for an analysis of the status of identity politics in the liberal polity. This is a significance that has not been explored in the contemporary literature. Pateman's account reveals very clearly why it has been so difficult for the liberal polity to accept and incorporate identity politics. Liberal theory specifies that identity does not belong in the public sphere; it is defined as private and thus politically illegitimate. Pateman focuses on the identity of women, an identity that is definitive of the private sphere, but her analysis applies to all private identities. Bringing identity into the liberal polity violates the basic tenet of the separation of public and private. The realm of the public is the realm of the abstract citizen. Bringing private identities into that realm entails violating the objectivity that abstraction ensures. The structure of the liberal polity contrasts the illegitimacy of identity politics with the legitimacy of the universal citizen.

But Pateman's analysis reveals another significant characteristic of this structure. The universal citizen has a hidden identity. He is both universal *and* masculine; the two are, in effect, synonymous in liberal theory.[6] The hidden identity of the universal citizen creates almost insuperable problems for identity politics. We are told that the citizen of liberalism is lacking in the specificities of identity that define the private sphere. Yet when certain identities try to enter the public sphere, we discover that there is, indeed, an identity requirement for that sphere: one must be a white male property owner; other identities are precisely that—other—and are not legitimate. In a sense the mere existence of identity politics proves this point. The participants in identity politics would not have organized politically unless they felt excluded from the polity. The veiled identity of the citizen of liberalism, however, dooms identity politics to failure. Identities are not appropriate in the public sphere, because the citizen is universal. Defining the identity of this citizen, and thus proclaim-

---

6. Pateman's point here is similar to Simone de Beauvoir's assertion that *masculine* and *feminine* are not symmetrical terms, because the masculine is both the positive and the neutral in this dichotomy (de Beauvoir 1972, 15).

ing the legitimacy of identity in the public sphere, are impossible because the veil of fraternity hides this identity from view.

In what follows I will elaborate on these arguments. But before leaving Pateman, I want to note another strength of her approach: her advocacy of the embodied citizen. Pateman argues that there is no neutral citizen/individual and thus that we must bring the specificities of our embodied identity into the political sphere. She further asserts that this entails a radically different political order. I think it is profoundly important to pursue this suggestion beyond the brief outline Pateman offers.[7] We need to define a politics in which identities are neither hidden nor illegitimate. But as Pateman's analysis so graphically reveals, realizing this vision entails nothing less than challenging the fundamentals of the liberal polity: the universal citizen and the public/private distinction on which it rests. Pateman's analysis reveals why identity politics has posed such a dilemma for liberalism. If we take it seriously, it entails a politics of identity and differences that transcends liberal assumptions.

Contemporary Liberal Identity

It is irrefutable that the classical liberal theorists were patriarchal, embodying the sexist assumptions of their day. But it could easily be argued, and, of course, has been, that these assumptions have been successfully challenged by contemporary liberalism. Women, nonwhite men, and non-property-owning males have been enfranchised. Liberalism today incorporates individuals of a wide variety. Even Rawls, whom Pateman identifies as embracing the patriarchal concept of the individual, grants equality to women.

In the following I will use the analysis developed in the previous section to argue for the contemporary relevance of Pateman's critique of liberalism. But my argument is not only that contemporary liberalism excludes women from the definition of the "individual." More broadly I argue that the separation between public and private that is at the heart of liberalism functions to exclude all "others" from the political sphere. The pattern that Pateman identified continues to hold true for contemporary liberalism. In theory liberalism excludes *all* particular identities from the public sphere. The political world is the world of abstract citizens who are free and equal. In practice, however, the abstract citizen has a very distinct identity: he is still the white male property owner. What this means is that although those who do not fit this category are al-

7. See Grosz 1994 and Gatens 1996 for other arguments for embodiment.

lowed into the public sphere, they enter as others, as those who, unlike the abstract citizen, possess identities.

The best way to establish this thesis is to examine the work of the quintessential twentieth-century liberal theorist, John Rawls. Rawls's reformulation of liberalism has been immensely influential in contemporary theory and practice. Furthermore, although *A Theory of Justice* (1971) was written before identity and multiculturalism became major political forces, in his more recent work Rawls has addressed these issues. His work as a whole, therefore, is a good place to start in the attempt to assess the role of identity in contemporary liberalism.

Rawls's discussion of the original position in *A Theory of Justice* conforms very neatly to Pateman's critique. The original position and the veil of ignorance that defines it are the central theoretical tools of Rawls's work. Although the parties in the original position are not explicitly defined as male, they are defined as heads of household which comes to much the same thing (Rawls 1971, 128). Furthermore, Rawls defines the veil of ignorance that characterizes these parties as ignorance of "his place in society, his class position or social status" (137). In his description and defense of the original position, Rawls appeals to Kant's ethics. He claims that the notion of the veil of ignorance is implicit in Kantian ethics and that "the parties in the original position are theoretically defined individuals" (147).

The reference to Kant here is revealing. More than that of any other modern philosopher, Kant's work provides the definitive expression of the rational, autonomous, abstract individual that is at the heart of modernism. That the parties in the original position are modeled after these Kantian individuals is clear. Rawls himself admits this. But I would like to suggest that the abstraction that characterizes the Kantian individual extends beyond the original position and the veil of ignorance that encompasses it. The veil of ignorance that characterizes the original position does not dissolve once the principles of justice are defined and political society is established. It remains in place as the division between what Rawls calls "public and nonpublic identity." For Rawls the particularities of an individual's identity have no place in the original position *or* in the public sphere; they are relegated to what he calls the individual's nonpublic identity.

Rawls does not ignore the psychological dimension of identity. He asserts that childhood development affects adult performance and that "[h]appy family and social circumstances" are necessary for the development of natural capacities (74). But it is significant that Rawls declines to pursue further what he labels "these complications" (301). Instead he wants to keep the veil firmly in place. The citizen that inhabits the public sphere of Rawls's liberal society is the abstract individual of Kantian ethics. The citizen's education, which, presumably, occurs in the family, is a Kantian education: "Thus moral education is education for autonomy" (516). The morality of principles that guides Rawls's liberal society is a morality divorced from the contingency of individual lives:

> Once a morality of principles is accepted, however, moral attitudes are no longer connected solely with the well-being and approval of particular chosen individuals and groups but are shaped by a conception of right chosen irrespective of these contingencies. Our moral sentiments display an independence from the accidental circumstances of our world, the meaning of this independence being given by the description of the original position in its Kantian interpretation. (475)

Carol Gilligan (1982) has argued that the Kantian morality of principles is a masculine morality, distinct from the care voice characteristic of the moral voice of women. Women are socialized to think in terms of context and contingency, men in terms of abstraction and autonomy.[8] This distinction characterizes the dichotomy between public and nonpublic identity that is central to Rawls's conception of the functioning of liberal society. It is the Kantian, masculine individual that inhabits the public sphere. The contingent feminine individual defines the nonpublic sphere. In *A Theory of Justice* Rawls declares that our "natural attachments" to particular persons and groups "still have an appropriate place" (1971, 475). In an article written in 1985, he defines this place more specifically. He insists that changes in an individual's conception of the good, presumably rooted in his/her nonpublic identity, will not effect the public identity of the citizen (1985, 241). He even concedes that "citizens may have and normally do have at any given time, affections, devotions, and loyalties that they believe they would not and indeed could and should not stand apart from and objectively evaluate from the point of view of their purely rational good" (241). They may regard it as unthinkable to define themselves apart from these beliefs. This, Rawls concludes, is their nonpublic identity (241). And it is this identity that has no place in the political sphere.

Rawls does not address issues of identity politics and multiculturalism in *A Theory of Justice*. If we want to assess his stance on identity, then, it is only fair to look at his later work, where he explicitly discusses these issues. In the in-

8. It is significant that Rawls looks to the moral psychologist Lawrence Kohlberg to establish the moral basis of his theory. It was in opposition to Kohlberg's theory that Gilligan formulated her own theory of the different moral voice of women.

troduction to *Political Liberalism,* Rawls asserts that his principal problem is to analyze how it is possible that there may exist over time a stable and just society of free and equal citizens profoundly divided by reasonable though incompatible religious and philosophical doctrines (1993, xvii). At the very outset, however, Rawls makes it clear that he has no intention of lifting the veil in order to allow differences into the public sphere. On the contrary, he asserts that the means by which political liberalism is established is by distinguishing the public point of view from nonpublic points of view (xix). Rawls even acknowledges the criticisms of his earlier book on the grounds that his conception of the individual cannot deal with gender and the family. He dismissively asserts that these difficulties can be overcome but that "I do not try to show in these lectures" how they might be (xxix).

Rawls's position on identity as it develops in *Political Liberalism* departs from that of *A Theory of Justice* in that he devotes more time to the interaction of what he calls a citizen's public and nonpublic identity. But his basic position remains unchanged. He deals with the problems raised by diversity with the same theoretical tools that defined *A Theory of Justice:* the original position and the veil of ignorance (23). And, as in *A Theory of Justice,* the veil that characterizes the original position remains in place after the formation of political society. It is, if anything, drawn more tightly. Rawls does discuss influences from the nonpublic sphere on the formation of identity. He states that society and culture's history are the means by which we find our place in the world (222). But the way in which he describes this influence is revealing: "*Among the elements* affecting the realization of natural capacities are social attitudes of encouragement and support and the institutions concerned with their training and use" (my emphasis). In addition, potential abilities are "not something unaffected by social forms and particular contingencies" (270). In other words, society, culture, and socialization are factors in individual development, but only factors; they are contingent, not constitutive. Rawls's clearest statement of this is his conclusion to his discussion: "[W]e are born into our society and within its framework realize but one of the many possible forms of our person" (277). It seems clear from this that Rawls presupposes an innate identity that will be shaped but not constituted by social influences. Far from abandoning the Kantian subject of his previous work, he is clarifying it.

If we look at Rawls's theory in *Political Liberalism* from the perspective of the place of the particularities of identity and their role in the public realm, nothing has changed here, from either *A Theory of Justice* or classical liberalism. The rational, disembodied individual is the only appropriate occupant of the public realm. All personal characteristics are relegated to a nonpublic identity and carefully screened from the public sphere. That these characteristics are not defined as constitutive is also clear: they are factors *among others* that shape individuals, not *the* factors. What Rawls leaves us with is a bifurcated individual: "For we always assume that citizens have two views, a comprehensive and a political view; and that their overall view can be divided into two parts, suitably related" (140). "Suitably related," it is clear, means that nonpublic identity is removed from public view.

Near the end of *Political Liberalism*, Rawls declares that there are many nonpublic reasons but only one public reason (200). The issue of public reason, a highly contested issue in the context of identity politics and multiculturalism, is the subject of a subsequent article, "The Idea of Public Reason Revisited" (Rawls 1999). As in *Political Liberalism*, Rawls begins with the assertion that a basic feature of democracy is the fact of a plurality of conflicting reasonable comprehensive doctrines. Rawls's thesis is that "in public reason comprehensive doctrines of truth or right be replaced by an idea of the politically reasonable addressed to citizens as citizens" (574). He defines the "public political forum" in which public reason would be expressed as composed of the discourse of judges, government officials, and candidates for public office (575).

None of this is new. We have the bifurcated individual divided into public and nonpublic selves; we have a single standard for public political discourse. What is notable in this context is that Rawls explicitly deals with the family and its relationship to political reason. His first point is that in a democratic regime the government has a legitimate interest in the family because of its role in reproducing political society over time (586). Here Rawls is in a long tradition of liberal and nonliberal thinkers in defining the family as politically significant because it produces future citizens. But, unlike theorists such as Rousseau, Rawls lives in a time when issues of the family and particularly women's role in the family are on the political agenda. Thus Rawls is compelled to address such issues.

Rawls begins by conceding that he did not devote enough attention to the issue of equal justice for women in *A Theory of Justice*. In a footnote, admitting that writers such as Susan Moller Okin have encouraged him to think about a liberal account of equal justice for women, he comments, "I have gained a great deal from their writings" (1999, 595n). But when it comes to developing a liberal account of equal justice for women, it does not appear that Rawls has done much thinking about this issue at all. Once more we get the disclaimer that "I cannot pursue these complexities here, but assume that as children we grow up in a small intimate group in which elders (normally parents) have a certain moral and political authority" (596). It emerges that the principle guiding Rawls's consideration of the family is that the principles of political justice do not apply to its internal life, but do impose essential constraints on the family as an institution and hence guarantee basic rights and liberties for all members.

This principle leads Rawls to a conclusion on the issue of the family that ignores the substance of all the feminist critiques of the family he claims to have studied: "Since wives are equal citizens with their husbands, they have all the same basic rights, liberties, and opportunities as their husbands; and this, together with the correct application of other principles of justice, suffices to secure their equality and independence" (597). As if this were not enough, Rawls then adds two more elements to his analysis that fly in the face of feminist critiques. First, he asserts, "But at some point society has to rely on the natural affection and goodwill of mature family members" (598). Second, he argues that a liberal conception of justice may have to allow for some traditional gendered division of labor in the family provided it is fully voluntary and does not result from or lead to injustice (599).

Rawls's position here explicitly contradicts arguments that have been the focus of feminist discussions for the past several decades. But after taking what amounts to an antifeminist position, Rawls then seems to turn against his own argument by following a suggestion made by Okin. He claims that if women's inequality is caused in large part by the unequal division of labor in the family then steps must be taken to "either equalize their share or compensate them for it" (600). But instead of addressing this provocative issue, Rawls once more issues a disclaimer: it is not the job of political philosophy to decide how to do this. The remedy for the "gender system's faults," he argues, depends on social theory and human psychology and much else. It cannot be settled by a conception of justice alone (601).

So, in the end, nothing really changes. Gender inequality is a problem of justice, but not one that Rawls's principles of justice must be concerned about. The veil remains in place. Women are citizens, and as citizens they are the same as everyone else. In defining citizens as citizens, Rawls concludes, "we don't view persons as socially situated or otherwise rooted" (607). Personal identity belongs in the nonpublic, not the public, realm. The Kantian abstract citizen remains at the center of liberalism.

It should go without saying that Rawls is not the only contemporary liberal to attempt to adapt liberalism to the new realities of identity politics and multiculturalism. I will make no attempt to offer a comprehensive review of this literature here. I have focused on Rawls because his liberalism has and continues to be a major influence in both theory and practice. It accords with the basic presuppositions of most citizens in liberal societies. This cannot be said for the redefinitions of liberalism that have emerged in recent years. But the work of these liberal theorists, and specifically their concern with diversity, are noteworthy. These theories represent an attempt to move beyond the presuppositions of liberalism and the abstract neutrality on which it is founded. The question remains, however, of to what extent liberalism can be stretched in the direction of diversity.

Some contemporary liberal thinkers have attempted to deal with diversity by arguing that liberalism can easily accommodate it. Thus Chandran Kukathas, like Rawls, argues that multiculturalism does not pose a problem for liberalism because "liberalism's counsel is to resist the demand for recognition (1998, 687). Liberalism, Kukathas asserts, is already fundamentally a theory of multiculturalism or pluralism. It asserts that diversity must be accommodated, that a unified community is impossible and undesirable. Liberalism, Kukathas concludes, "promotes no particular individual or individual interests"; it "might well be described as the politics of indifference" (691). Although he recognizes the objection that the politics of indifference will result in the domination of the standards of the dominant culture, he does not take this objection seriously. Underlying Kukathas's view is his assertion that groups or communities have no special moral primacy but, rather, are voluntary associations. It follows that, from a liberal point of view, people should be free to live according to the practices of their community because they should be free to associate, not because the culture has a right to be preserved (1992, 116).[9]

Other contemporary liberals, however, have taken diversity more seriously. Stuart Hampshire, for example, argues that in the face of diversity we can look only to procedures to secure any universal agreement. He argues: "Fairness and justice in procedures are the only virtues that can reasonably be considered as setting norms to be universally respected" (2000, 53). Andrea Baumeister summarizes this position when she argues that "the central challenge for liberals today is not to find grounds for universal rational agreement, but to develop a set of institutions which can effectively manage the conflict and antagonism that inevitably encompasses diversity" (2000, 200).

What is happening in these redefinitions of liberalism is that the neutrality and abstraction that characterize both classical and Rawlsian liberalism are being gradually eroded. This is significant. But it is also significant that these qualities have not been entirely abandoned. A further erosion occurs in the work of other liberal thinkers. Richard Flathman, for example, argues that liberalism has never been a closely integrated or firmly fixed doctrine. To define and defend his version of liberalism, Flathman looks to theorists who even he admits are not usually considered liberals. Among those he cites are Wittgenstein, Oakeshott, William James, Schopenhauer, Nietzsche, Sartre, and Arendt. In

9. See also Larmore 1987, Barry 2001.

defense of his position Flathman argues that it is not a question of whether these thinkers are liberals, but, rather, whether their ideas can strengthen liberal theory and practice (1992, 131). At the root of Flathman's liberalism is what he calls the "Liberal Principle": "It is a prima facie good for persons to form, to act on, and to satisfy and achieve desires and interests, objectives and purposes" (1989, 6). Since it is obvious that different persons will have different desires and interests, it follows that liberalism is, by definition, a theory of diversity.

Attempts to accommodate diversity in these redefinitions of liberalism, in short, form a continuum from denying that it is a problem to embracing it. Those, like Kukathas, who argue for liberalism's indifference deny the point made so forcibly by Pateman that liberalism is grounded in a very particular favoritism and that this favoritism is endemic to the liberal polity. But Pateman's critique is also relevant to the liberalisms on the other end of the continuum. In even the most pluralistic, diversity-conscious forms of liberalism there is still an unexamined commitment to the liberal individual and all that this entails. Flathman, for one, is very clear about this. The primary unit in thought and evaluation, he claims, is the individual (1989, 8). This individual, furthermore, has a rational life plan, a set of desires and goals on which he [*sic*] acts. What is missing in even the new liberalism is an acknowledgment that, in our society, this individual is gendered masculine. The rationality and autonomy that define him have been and continue to be defined in masculine terms. Furthermore, the rational life plan that this individual possesses is, for many persons, an alien conception. It is only "normal" for certain kinds of people in particular circumstances (Walker 1998, 136). Once more, "others" are not accommodated even in these new versions of liberalism.

This literature also raises a semantic question: how far can we extend the concept "liberal" before it becomes meaningless? If everyone is, finally, a liberal, then what meaning does the term retain? Maybe we should stop using the term altogether if we have stretched it so far from its original meaning. William Galston's *Liberal Pluralism: The Implications of Value Pluralism for Political Theory and Practice* (2002) is one of the recent attempts to redefine liberalism as compatible with pluralism. At the end of the book Galston states: "When we are trying to decide what to do, we are typically confronted with a multiplicity of worthy principles and genuine goals that are not neatly ordered and that cannot be translated into a common measure of value. This is not ignorance but, rather, the fact of the matter" (131). In *The Postmodern Condition* (1984), Lyotard advances a thesis that is strikingly similar to that of Galston. My point is not that postmodernism and liberalism are the same (although Richard Rorty seems to be claiming this) but, rather, that liberalism becomes a meaningless concept if it can accommodate almost any position.

I applaud the effort of contemporary liberals to accommodate diversity. The thesis of this book is that we must take the risk of difference, that we must challenge the neutrality and abstraction at the heart of liberalism. My points here are, first, that we must be careful not to sneak the abstract individual in through the back door without acknowledging his gendered character. Women, and many other "others," are not and cannot be "individuals" in the liberal sense of the term. Second, I am arguing that maybe we should stop calling what we have left after we have accommodated diversity "liberalism." Maybe this effort has created something else entirely and we should acknowledge this transformation.

My third point is that none of these authors seriously considers the feminist critique of the liberal individual. Rawls's failure to do so is not surprising. He is of a generation that was not exposed to feminist ideas. But these authors write in a time when feminism is more prominent in the academic world. Their failure to incorporate the feminist critique illustrates the point I am trying to make here: the revolutionary nature of this critique has not been realized.

The fact that this failure extends to contemporary feminist defenses of liberalism, however, is not only surprising but also disappointing. In the writings of contemporary liberal feminists, Pateman's arguments, if they are mentioned at all, are quickly dismissed. They are certainly not regarded as major impediments to the formulation of any feminist liberalism. Martha Nussbaum's work illustrates this attitude most clearly. Nussbaum argues explicitly that her goal is to refute the feminist critique of liberalism. Her work is solidly grounded in classical liberal values: the assertion that all human beings have dignity and equal worth. She argues that feminism's contribution to liberalism is to argue that sex is a morally irrelevant characteristic. Central to her argument is her defense of a universal human nature. Her thesis is that the concept of human nature that grounds liberalism, liberal individualism, does not entail egoism. It is thus compatible with the emphasis on care and love proposed by many contemporary feminists (1999, 10).

Nussbaum employs these principles to refute the feminist critique of liberalism. She asserts that the feminist dismissal of liberalism as too abstract is unfounded. Liberalism aims at equality of capabilities, she asserts, not abstract equality that ignores the historical setting (68). But when she turns to another aspect of the feminist critique, the claim that liberalism abstracts from birth, class, gender, and ethnicity, Nussbaum defends the abstraction. It is unwise, she states, to jettison the liberal account of human essence in favor of an account that gives more centrality to "accidental" features of religion, class, or gender. She writes: "Feminism needs to operate with a general notion of the human core, without forgetting that this core has been differently situated and also shaped in different times and places" (71).

Nussbaum's Kantian allegiances are very clear here. It is the rational, abstract chooser that must be the focus of moral and political deliberations, not the accidental features of race, class, and gender. But Nussbaum's most telling defense is her reply to the claim that any notion of universal human nature is necessarily hierarchical or enshrines masculine qualities as human. She asserts, "It is far from clear what this objection shows" (38). Nussbaum makes no attempt to address Pateman's argument that the "individual" of liberal theory is inherently masculine. Nor does she attempt to refute Pateman's claim that, far from offering a nonhierarchical, neutral conception of identity, liberalism establishes one identity as hegemonic; all others are at the same time illegitimate and inferior.[10]

Nussbaum's defense of liberalism remains solidly within the theoretical boundaries of liberal theory. A very different attempt to rescue liberalism from a feminist perspective is offered by Susan Moller Okin. Okin focuses her analysis specifically on the work of Rawls. She identifies both advantages and disadvantages in Rawls's liberal perspective. Like Pateman, Okin assumes that our legal and political system assumes that "individuals" are male heads of households (1989, 7). She further believes that the dichotomy on which this definition is based, the separation of public and private, is "artificial" (23). But she nevertheless maintains that "a consistent and wholehearted application of Rawls's liberal principles of justice can lead us to challenge fundamentally the gender system of society" (89). She intends to accomplish this by recasting the original position as the perspective of everybody rather than nobody (101).

Okin's critique of Rawls's neglect of gender is insightful. She faults him for not recognizing what many feminists call the social construction of gender, particularly as it operates in the family. Her argument for the perspective of everybody entails that men could imagine what she calls the standpoint of women and vice versa. A fully humanist theory of justice, she maintains, cannot be achieved without a critique of the public/domestic dichotomy (111). In short, for Okin as for many feminists, the personal is political. Yet there are also significant areas of agreement between Okin and Rawls on gender issues. Even in Okin's revised original position we must "imagine ourselves, as far as possible, in the original position, knowing neither what our sex nor any other personal characteristics will be once the veil of ignorance is lifted" (174). Although she concedes (in a footnote) that given the "deep effects of gender on our psy-

---

10. In *Women and Human Development* (2000), Nussbaum identifies her capabilities approach with Rawls's primary goods.

chologies," this will be a difficult task, she maintains that we should nevertheless try. Finally, and most tellingly, "[a] just future would be one without gender" (1989, 171).

Okin's attempt to reformulate Rawls's theory along feminist lines produces an odd and, ultimately, unworkable mix. Okin's critique of the public/private distinction is a central aspect of her theory. But without the public/private distinction, Rawls's theory makes no sense. Unless one can distinguish between public and nonpublic identity the principles of justice cannot be formulated. Okin's dismissal of this dichotomy thus entails a dismissal of Rawls's liberalism itself. Further, despite her advocacy of gender as an integral part of a theory of justice, Okin herself seems ambivalent about the role of gender in human life. While arguing strongly for the personal as political and the political effects of women's gender socialization, she takes back as much as she gives. She retains a genderless original position and, most significant, argues for the ideal of a genderless society. This society would be produced by the dual parenting that would solve the problems created by gender socialization in contemporary families. What her critique implies is that in our present unfortunate circumstances gender is a factor in politics, but that once we rectify the gender inequality in our society we can and should return to the genderless ideal of liberalism. The public/private dichotomy is thus reinstated.[11]

In the foregoing analysis of contemporary liberalism my goal has been to understand the role of identity in the contemporary liberal polity. The analysis leads to three conclusions. First, identity is both denied and established in the liberal polity. The universal citizen is defined as lacking a particular identity, yet behind this theoretical veil the hegemony of the white male property owner was (and is) firmly established. My argument has been that the most influential twentieth-century version of liberalism, that of Rawls, is rooted in this concept of the citizen and that it is implicit even in the redefinitions of liberalism that have been advanced in recent years. Second, identity politics constitutes a radical challenge to liberal politics in that it attempts to bring excluded identities into the political arena. The presence of these identities reveals the identity of the universal citizen; it tears down the veil behind which he hides. Tearing away the veil, further, brings the personal into the political sphere; it violates the public/private dichotomy at the center of liberalism. Identity politics thus is fundamentally illegitimate in the liberal polity. As Pateman correctly notes, the embodied individual does not fit into the liberal polity; the effort to make her do so has the potential to fundamentally change that polity.

11. Okin's argument in *Is Multiculturalism Bad for Women?* (1999) reinforces this position. Here she defends the universalism of liberalism specifically against the diversity of cultures.

My third conclusion is that this potential has not been realized; the theoretical structure of the liberal polity prevents it. Because of the veiled identity
at the center of the liberal polity, other identities can enter the political sphere
only *as* other. There is room for only two entities in the liberal polity: the "normal" citizen and the other. The identity of citizens who are not normal must
necessarily be fixed: they are others of different varieties but they are always
defined in contrast to the norm of the "universal" citizen. Thus women, gay
men, lesbians, African Americans, Native Americans, and so on, *have* an identity: they are other. White men, however, do not. This is graphically illustrated in contemporary politics in the United States in which various others
are trotted onto the political stage as a prelude to the arrival of the "real" political actors around whom the action revolves. The potential of identity politics to radically transform the liberal polity thus has been thwarted. What
has happened instead is that identity politics has been shaped to fit the parameters of liberalism.

Multiculturalism: A New Politics of Identity?

If, as I have argued, the veiled identity of the "universal citizen" of liberalism
dooms identity politics to failure in the liberal polity, then the next question
must be, How can we move toward a polity of embodied citizens? From the
perspective of contemporary political theory it would seem that the answer to
this question has already been formulated. The advent of multiculturalism in
both political theory and practice appears to be the perfect answer to the challenge of identity politics. Unlike liberals, multiculturalists claim to place identity at the center of politics. The whole point of multiculturalism is to bring
identities, and particularly previously excluded identities, into the political arena
as equal citizens.

The most prominent contemporary advocate of multiculturalism is Will
Kymlicka. In a series of books and articles Kymlicka argues strongly for a state
in which cultural membership is a central aspect of political life and citizenship. Most important, Kymlicka argues that this can be effected within the general framework of liberalism. Kymlicka places his argument for multiculturalism within the context of the liberal/communitarian debate that has occupied
political theorists for several decades. Kymlicka wants to make it clear from
the outset that he is not siding with the communitarians against liberalism.
Kymlicka specifically attacks the communitarian view of the self, arguing that
it is mistaken in fundamental respects. He characterizes the communitarian
view as one in which the individual cannot stand back and decide not to oc-

cupy the roles he/she has been assigned (1989, 57). This all-encompassing view of cultural membership is, Kymlicka argues, unacceptable and incoherent.

But it is also clear that Kymlicka wants to find a middle ground between this all-encompassing communitarian self and the abstract self of liberalism. His attempt to do so involves him in some interesting theoretical acrobatics. The first aspect of his argument, however, is historical. He asserts that the concept of group-differentiated rights had a prominent place in nineteenth- and twentieth-century liberalism. He notes that in their governing of the colonies, the British had to revise their universal theories to accommodate minority cultures in these societies. He then traces how these policies were overturned in the twentieth century (1995, 50–58). The implication, however, is clear: the attempt to incorporate cultural membership into the liberal polity has a specific historical precedent.

The core of Kymlicka's argument, however, is theoretical. He begins by conceding that there seems to be no room in the "moral ontology" of liberalism for the idea of collective rights (1989, 140). It is this theoretical position that Kymlicka seeks to challenge. His basic position is that "[i]ndividual and collective rights cannot compete for the same moral space in liberal theory since the value of the collective derives from its contribution to the value of individual lives" (140). Liberals, Kymlicka argues, have viewed the idea of collective rights for minority cultures as theoretically incoherent and practically dangerous (144). Against this Kymlicka argues that neither is the case. Using the example of aboriginal people in Canada, Kymlicka claims that the loss of cultural membership can and does have a devastating effect on the individual. He then generalizes this argument to assert that members of minority cultural communities face disadvantages whose rectification requires and justifies the provision of minority rights (163).

At this point in his argument Kymlicka makes an important theoretical leap: he enlists Rawls in defense of his position: "Rawls's own argument for the importance of liberty as a primary good is also an argument for the importance of cultural membership as a primary good (166). Kymlicka then concludes: "The notion of respect for persons *qua* members of cultures based on the recognition and importance of the primary good of cultural membership is not, therefore, an illiberal one" (167).

This is a very bold theoretical move. Kymlicka is challenging what most liberals (as he himself concedes) define as the core of liberalism: the primacy of the individual over the group. Despite the centrality of this belief, Kymlicka argues that challenging it does not challenge liberalism itself. But Kymlicka goes even further: he wants to subsume his position under the rubric of a very specific form of liberal theory, Rawlsian liberalism. The reference to "primary

goods" here is unambiguous. Kymlicka wants to argue that cultural membership can and should be defined as one of the primary goods that persons in the
original position would want to pursue. Cultural membership, Kymlicka argues, is a central aspect of our essential interest in leading a good life (168). It
follows that a government that gives special rights to members of a distinct
cultural community may still be treating them as individuals. The provision
of rights merely reflects a "different view" of how to treat them as individuals
and as equals (211). This leads Kymlicka to advocate what he calls "group-
differentiated citizenship," a model based on the idea that "justice between
groups requires that members of different groups be accorded different rights"
(1995, 47).

The "different view" that Kymlicka advocates hinges on his definition of cultural membership. Kymlicka wants to incorporate cultural membership into liberalism by making it compatible with the individualism that constitutes liberal
theory. The result of his effort is an incoherent view of identity as well as a
redefinition of liberalism that constitutes a significant departure from its original meaning.. To understand Kymlicka's conception of cultural membership, it
is important to begin with his assertion that his conception is distinct from that
of the communitarians. While the communitarian self is determined by culture,
the self Kymlicka presents is *enabled* by culture: "membership in a cultural community is what enables individual freedom, what enables meaningful choices
about how to lead one's life" (1989, 200). Cultural membership "affects one's
sense of personal identity and capacity" (175). It is the "context within which
we choose our ends and come to see their value" (192). One of the most controversial aspects of Kymlicka's definition is his argument that as a culture is
liberalized, members of the culture question traditional values, and cultural identity becomes "thinner" (1995, 87). He asserts that people can stand back and assess the moral values of a traditional way of life and should be given the legal
right to do so (92). In the "thinner" version of cultural membership that characterizes liberal societies, presumably, this process of assessment is pervasive.

Although at one point Kymlicka refers to "the constitutive nature of our
cultural identity" (1989, 176), this is not the main thrust of his theory of identity. Identity, for Kymlicka, is about choice. Although culture "affects" us, it
does not define identity. We can stand back from it; it is only one of the elements that constitute us. Kymlicka summarizes his position on the relationship between identity and culture at the end of *Liberalism, Community, and Culture*. Liberalism, he concludes, offers us a

> very plausible and compelling account of community and culture. It
> recognizes the way that communal and cultural aspects of social life

provide the possibility for, and locus of, the pursuit of human values. But it also insists that these values, like most important values, ultimately depend on the way that each individual understands and evaluates them. The value of the communal and cultural aspects of our existence depends, to a large degree, on the way that individuals form and revise attachments and projects around those features of our social life. Hence that value of the "social" depends on, rather than conflicts with, the "individualistic" picture of people forming and pursuing their own understanding of the good. (1989, 253–54)

Kymlicka's individual is essentially the individual of liberalism only with culture thrown in as one of the primary goals that the individual pursues. This individual represents an attempt to integrate two incompatible theories of identity. One theory, that defined by object relations theory among others, is relational; the self is not pregiven but formed in relation to significant others; it is a self constituted by cultural context. The second theory is that of the modernist subject, the pregiven, rational autonomous chooser of the liberal tradition. Kymlicka's self partakes of aspects of both theories. His self is culturally constituted, a being for whom culture is a primary good. But his self is also a rational chooser who can step back and assess his/her cultural context. On the first theory of identity, however, there is no place from which the self can do this assessing; on the second theory of identity there is no need to do so, because culture is not constitutive. Kymlicka wants to have his cake and eat it too. He wants to retain the liberal, choosing individual without denying the constitutive nature of culture. The result is incoherence.

We have encountered this individual before. Linda Alcoff, among others, has attempted a similar integration of elements of the modernist and, in her case, the discursive subject. My contention is that these attempts at integration do not work. If, as the object relations theorists argue, identity is formed relationally, then we must reject the modernist subject in its totality. Kymlicka is not willing to do this, probably because, like Alcoff, he assumes that doing so entails that we must accept the self as monolithically determined by culture. This assumption is unfounded. The goal in the following chapter is to develop a refutation of this assumption.

It is difficult to evaluate Kymlicka's claim that his version of multiculturalism is compatible with liberalism. Cultural membership in classical liberalism is in the private, nonpublic realm. Bringing it into the public realm violates the basis of this liberalism. Kymlicka's theory is also incompatible with the Rawlsian version of liberalism under which Kymlicka would like to subsume it. Primary goods are, first, the result of rational choice. This does not apply to cultural membership. We do not choose our cultural identity; it is something we are born into. Second, primary goods are generic and neutral. The honor, dignity, equality and respect that define the abstract, Kantian subject are universal. Cultural membership, by contrast, is specific and particular. As Kant makes so clear, it has no place in the sphere of the abstract individual.

Yet Kymlicka insists that his theory is compatible with liberalism. This claim brings us back to the question of how far we can stretch the concept "liberalism" and retain a coherent definition. I will not try to answer this question. Instead, I assert that, if we are to define a new politics of identity, what we must start with is a new theory of identity. Retaining aspects of the modernist subject in order to retain the label *liberalism* is not a productive strategy. Identity politics entails a transformation of the basic concepts of liberalism. Acknowledging this should be the basis of any attempt to define the politics of identity. Kymlicka's multicultural liberalism does not accomplish this goal.

Kymlicka is not the only multiculturalist writing today. Other multiculturalists have moved away from liberalism and have begun to explore the radical implications entailed by multiculturalism and identity politics. Charles Taylor (1994) is less concerned than Kymlicka with adapting multiculturalism to liberalism. But Taylor and Kymlicka share one important conviction: that the recognition of one's cultural membership is a vital human need and thus that this need must be met by democratic governments. In advancing this argument Taylor is building on the theory of identity he developed in *Sources of the Self*. His thesis is that our identity is partly shaped by recognition or its absence. Thus individuals can suffer real damage if society mirrors back to them a demeaning identity (1994, 25). Informing this thesis is Taylor's conviction that identity is fundamentally dialogic in character: "Thus my discovery of my own identity doesn't mean I work it out in isolation, but that I negotiate it through dialogue, partly overt, partly internal, with others" (34).

Taylor's account has the virtue of clarifying a fundamental contrast between liberalism and multiculturalism that Kymlicka was at pains to deny: the different concepts of identity that inform each. Multiculturalism replaces the abstract neutral citizen of liberalism with the relational self that is particular and contextual. Taylor's dialogic identity affirms this self; this is the self theorized by object relations theory. What Taylor makes clear is that this self necessitates a politics beyond liberalism, a politics that eschews neutrality and abstraction. His politics of recognition is an attempt to define that new politics.

That the politics of recognition represents a significant departure from liberalism is clear. The advent of multiculturalism in both theory and practice is a positive move in the direction of defining a politics of identity, a politics of embodied citizens. I will rely on many multiculturalist theorists in my own attempt to define that politics. But multiculturalism represents only the first step in the process of defining a new politics of identity. It is not the only option for that politics. Multiculturalism raises a number of serious political questions that identity politics must address. What does recognition entail? Can it be legislated? Does recognition occur in the political arena? The social? The familial? How do we combat the demeaning identity that Taylor discusses? Another set of issues arises around the question of how group recognition would be realized. What groups should be recognized, granted a particular political status, or both? Would citizens be forced to identify themselves as members of one group rather than another? It is my contention, first, that these questions must be addressed if we are to be clear about what the new politics of identity entails and, second, that many multicultural theorists ignore these issues. In the following, I will look at the work of a number of multiculturalist theorists who address these questions in useful ways.

Iris Marion Young's "politics of difference" (1989, 1990, 1997, 2000) is a significant contribution to the debate over multiculturalism. Young begins with the presupposition that a democratic public should provide mechanisms for the effective representation and recognition of the constituent groups that are oppressed and disadvantaged by it (1989, 261). Her thesis is that group representation is the best means to promote just outcomes in the democratic decision-making process. How this might be accomplished is the subject of *Justice and the Politics of Difference* (1990).

Young makes it clear from the outset that the politics of difference requires both a new conception of politics and a new conception of the individual. She declares that she is seeking a concept of justice that is defined not in terms of distribution, but in terms of domination and oppression. She finds it in what she calls "situated political reflection," a politics that recognizes rather than represses difference. The result is an "enabling" conception of justice that refers "to the institutional conditions necessary for the development and exercise of individual capacities and collective communication and cooperation" (39). Central to this conception is Young's definition of the social group: "a collective of persons differentiated from at least one other group by cultural forms, practices, or ways of life" (43).

In an argument that parallels that of Pateman, Young asserts that the ideal of impartiality in moral theory expresses a logic of identity that reduces differences to unity and masks the particular perspective of dominant groups. Against this Young argues for the ideal of a "heterogenous public in which persons stand forth with their differences acknowledged and respected" (119). The politics of difference Young advocates requires different treatment for different groups, sometimes even according special treatment to particular groups

(158). She concludes that a politics that asserts the positivity of group differences is liberatory and empowering (166).

Young's account, like Taylor's, clarifies the difference entailed by the politics of difference. Bringing difference into politics radically changes liberalism. It challenges the alleged neutrality of liberal politics. But Young's greatest contribution is that she explores a problem that is central to the politics of difference: the relationship between identity and group membership. Young wants to affirm the political necessity of group membership while avoiding the inevitable problems it entails. Thus she wants to assert that group meanings partially constitute individual identities while at the same time avoiding the fixing of identity that is the greatest danger of identity politics. Her solution is to assert that individuals can reject group identity, that people are heterogenous, and that we should learn to be comfortable with this heterogeneity. The politics of difference, she asserts, does not define difference as essential, but as the result of the process of social forces (1990, 153–57). On her account, groups are ambiguous, relational, shifting (171). In recognition of the importance of this issue, Young returns to it in subsequent work. She develops the thesis that group membership can best be understood in terms of Sartre's concept of seriality (1994, 1997). A series is a social collective whose members are unified passively by the relations their actions have to material objects and practices—inert histories (1997, 27). Using this perspective Young can define group identity as inessential, shifting, and relational.

Young's account is an important contribution to the definition of the politics of difference. In order to advocate such a politics we must have a clear account of how identity relates to group membership. We need to avoid the fixing of identity that is the Achilles heel of identity politics. Although Young's account has the virtue of acknowledging the difficulty of defining group membership politically, more work must be done to avoid the problems this entails. Defining groups inessentially is an important first step, but only a first step. Defining the subsequent steps will be the subject of the next chapter.

Another significant indictment of liberalism from a multicultural perspective is that of Bhikher Parekh (2000). Parekh attacks the alleged neutrality of liberalism by arguing that liberalism is a substantive doctrine advocating a specific view of man and society and producing a distinct way of life. As a consequence, he asserts, it cannot provide an impartial framework to conceptualize other cultures and their relations with it. Parekh further argues that the modern (liberal) state is preoccupied with political and cultural homogeneity, a characteristic inherent in the state itself (184). Parekh's conclusion is that since we can neither write off the state nor continue with it in its present form, we need to reconceptualize its nature and role (194). What he proposes is a "community of communities" and a new concept of equality based in difference rather than sameness (240).

Parekh's multiculturalism, like that of Young, is very clear about the radical implications of the multicultural challenge to liberalism. There are two aspects of his approach that are particularly valuable, aspects that I will build on in my own approach to a new politics of identity. First, Parekh argues that equal rights do not mean identical rights, that equality of opportunity exists only if individuals possess the capacity to exercise it (240–41). Most pointedly he argues that there is no single principle in terms of which disputed practices can be evaluated (267). This thesis not only violates the basis of liberalism, it points toward a new definition of politics in which difference rather than (alleged) neutrality is the central principle. Like Young, Parekh makes it clear that a politics of difference entails that one of the pillars of the liberal state, a universal standard for all citizens, must be challenged.

The second aspect of Parekh's thought I want to build on is his assertion near the end of his book that for the protection of the rights of communities, law is a "blunt instrument." He argues that we should rely not just on the law but also on other forms of pressure: public opinion, sanctions, and so forth (316). I will take up this point extensively in the last chapter. Here I just want to argue that the new politics of identity demands a new definition of politics that challenges the public/private distinction at the heart of liberalism in two respects. Not only does the new politics of identity bring private identities into the public realm, but it also redefines the public/political to include more than the realm of laws. Power is everywhere; it must be met everywhere. This entails that we must develop a more inclusive conception of political action that, as Parekh argues, transcends the strictly legal sphere.

Another aspect of the multicultural challenge to liberalism is addressed in the work of Monique Deveaux. In *Cultural Pluralism and Dilemmas of Justice* (2000) Deveaux argues for what she calls "deliberative liberalism." Although she claims that her position is not a wholesale rejection of liberalism, the elements of her argument for the political significance of group-based social differences constitute a radical departure from key liberal assumptions. The main target of Deveaux's critique is the neutrality liberals and their position on multiculturalism. She argues that defining difference in terms of toleration, neutrality, and assimilation is problematic and is "unlikely" to secure equal justice for cultural minorities in democratic states (35, 66). Like many multiculturalists, Deveaux argues that liberalism errs in defining difference in individual terms. We can only secure equal justice, Deveaux asserts, if we define difference collectively (30).

Although variants of this position have been argued by many multiculturalists, Deveaux's approach contains a unique element. In her critique of neutrality liberals, she argues that the values of neutral justification and the public/private distinction may not, as they assume, be universally shared. Rawlsian, neutral liberalism limits the kinds of reasons that can be used in the public sphere. Only reasons based on universal, abstract principles are appropriate. This restriction, Deveaux argues, may not be acceptable to many minority cultural groups (67). The claims of minority groups for cultural recognition cannot be articulated in terms of neutral, public reasons (94). Deveaux concludes: "Decision-making styles of minority groups frequently conflict with dominant liberal models of deliberation; demands for respect and political inclusion may require that some of these differences be accommodated" (175).

This is a profoundly important point. What Deveaux's analysis reveals is that identity politics challenges yet one more aspect of the public/private distinction that informs liberalism. Deveaux argues that this distinction results in the exclusion of particularistic reasons from the public sphere. Only certain kinds of reasons are appropriate in the public sphere of the liberal polity: abstract, universal principles that are divorced from particular contexts or persons. Although she does not make this connection, this definition of the public sphere accords with what since Carol Gilligan has been called the justice voice. Gilligan's point is that the abstraction and universality of the justice voice is foreign to women. Deveaux is arguing that it is foreign to many cultural minorities as well.[12]

Challenging the dominance of the justice voice in the public sphere completely alters the structure of the liberal polity. Central to the justice voice is the reliance on a single, universal standard that applies equally to all. Opening up discourse in the public sphere to the personal and the particular challenges this universal standard. Parekh argues that this necessitates multiple standards of judgment. Deveaux's position leads to a related conclusion: different "decision-making styles" must be accommodated. Challenging the justice voice radically alters the public sphere, opening it to reasons and discourses that neutral liberals have excluded as "unreasonable."

The goal of my discussion of these multiculturalist theorists has been to highlight the contrast between multiculturalism and liberalism. With the notable exception of Kymlicka, multiculturalists acknowledge that embracing a politics of identity entails abandoning the central tenets of liberalism. Bringing identity into the public sphere tears away the veil of impartiality that masks the partiality of the universal citizen. It challenges the notion that equality

---

12. Tully makes a similar point (1995, 173). Sanders (1997) and Young (1996) present critiques of deliberative democracy that emphasizes the hegemony of rational argument.

defined as equal treatment is the essence of political justice. It introduces the radical idea that a just politics can and should abandon a single standard of judgment. It rejects the concept of "reasonable argument" as exclusively defined by abstract, universal principles. Finally, the multiculturalists' assertion that groups, not individuals, have rights challenges the individualism at the heart of liberalism.

In the following I will build on many of these arguments that are advanced by the multiculturalists discussed above. I want to stress, however, that if we accept the relational subject of object relations theory and try to craft a politics that corresponds to this subject, it does not necessarily follow that our only option is the politics outlined by the multiculturalists. Multiculturalists have revealed the liabilities of the liberal polity and pointed in the direction of a very different political order. But multiculturalism, far from providing a blueprint for a new politics of identity, has only begun the difficult process of defining the parameters that politics must take. Precisely because a politics of identity entails such a radical departure from liberalism, the elements of that politics require a careful definition. Specifically, there are three central issues that must be explored: replacing the abstract citizen with the embodied citizen, defining the relationship between identity and group membership, and formulating a redefinition of politics that deconstructs the public/private dichotomy.

I address the problem of replacing the abstract citizen with the embodied citizen in the following section by expanding on suggestions made by Young, Parekh, and Deveaux. One of the sacred cows of liberalism is the universal standard by which all citizens are judged. What happens when we remove this universal standard and even challenge the necessity of such a standard? Doing so entails bringing the embodied citizen into the political/legal process. My argument is that there are elements in contemporary politics that are moving in this direction, but they have made little headway against the dominant tradition of universality.

The second problem, defining the relationship between identity and group membership, is central to the understanding of the dynamics of identity politics. Yet it is a problem that most multiculturalists gloss over or ignore entirely. If they deal with it at all, they assume given group identities that constitute societies. This is a dangerous assumption. Unless it is challenged, we cannot avoid the fixing of identities that is the most problematic aspect of identity politics. An array of questions arise: Can we assume that everyone in a particular group can or should be classified under a single identity? Do individuals choose to identify with specific groups or is that identity assigned to them? Can individuals change group identifications? How do we account for the heterogeneity of identities in any individual? How can we accommodate legitimate group needs without reifying the identity of particular groups?

The multiculturalist who is most concerned with this problem is Iris Marion Young. Group identities, Young argues, are inessential, shifting. Individuals can reject the group identities assigned to them and embrace others. But even Young's theory leaves a number of key questions unanswered: How do we reject group identities? Where does resistance come from? Why do some individuals resist and others not? To what extent are we defined by group identities? How and why can this change over time? Solving this problem will be the major concern of the following chapter. My argument focuses on the distinction between public and private identity. My thesis is that unless we are clear about this distinction, we cannot be clear about what a politics of difference entails.

I address the third problem, a redefinition of politics that deconstructs the public/private distinction, in the final chapter. Parekh suggested that in matters of identity law is a "blunt instrument," that in order to confront discrimination we must move beyond the strictly legal/political sphere. My argument elaborates on this suggestion. Relying on the work of Foucault, I argue for a more encompassing definition of power and politics in society.

Beyond Uniformity

> The members of a political association aim, by their very
> nature, at being equal and differing in nothing.
>
>   —Aristotle, *The Politics*

> A picture held us captive. And we could not get outside it, for
> it lay in our language and language seemed to repeat it to us
> inexorably.
>
>   —Wittgenstein, *Philosophical Investigations*

In his discussion of the history of modern constitutionalism and its implications for multiculturalism, James Tully quotes the preceding passage from Wittgenstein to describe the force of the ideas that inform this concept. His thesis is that modern constitutionalism has tended toward a language of uniformity that makes recognition of cultural diversity impossible (Tully 1995, 58). It is this language of uniformity, Tully argues, that holds us captive, setting the stage for the rejection of the demand for cultural recognition. Tully's historical analysis reveals why this picture has been so powerful. In the seventeenth century it replaced what he calls the "ancient" constitution based on tradition and custom. Thus the uniformity at the heart of liberal constitutionalism was, from the outset, defined as liberatory. It freed human beings from the bonds of tradition that defined individuals by status and class.

The uniformity of modern constitutionalism, then, has since its inception defined justice as impartiality and, conversely, defined injustice as partiality. Any reference to diversity is necessarily associated with a retreat to the discrimination and injustice that characterized the past. Custom and culture are defined as the enemies of progress and reason (88). Like Pateman, Tully wants to expose this impartiality as the partiality of the hegemonic group. He argues that what he calls the "feigned cultural indifference" of constitutionalism reinforces the dominant male culture at the expense of all others. And, like Taylor, he argues that the recognition and protection of cultural diversity is a necessary condition of the primary good of self-respect (191).

Commenting on the politics of difference, Cornell West remarks: "Distinctive features of the new cultural politics of difference are: to trash the monolithic and homogeneous in the name of diversity, multiplicity and heterogeneity; to reject the abstract, general and universal in light of the concrete, specific and particular; and to historicize, contextualize and pluralize by highlighting the contingent, provisional, variable, tentative, shifting and changing" (1995, 147). West's comments clarify why the politics of identity/difference has been so problematic in the culture of liberalism. A picture has held us captive. That picture tells a story in which diversity equals discrimination and uniformity equals justice. It has been my argument in the foregoing that identity politics profoundly challenges the liberal polity. It calls for a politics of diversity rather than uniformity, a politics of embodied citizens and multiple standards. This politics has not succeeded in transforming liberalism, because it challenges deeply held convictions at the root of the liberal polity, convictions embedded in our political language.

The area where the threat of difference and diversity looms largest is the law. The law is the pillar of liberal constitutionalism. All citizens are equal before the law. Law is blind; the statue in front of the United States Supreme Court building in Washington, D.C., is blindfolded. To introduce difference into the law, to jettison the universal standard in favor of a multiplicity of standards appears to invite chaos. Worse, it threatens to return us to the discrimination of the past. But the law is also the area of our public life where the partiality that Pateman and others have revealed is most evident. At the root of our legal system is the abstract citizen, offering a uniform standard by which everyone is judged equally. But behind the veil of impartiality, this abstract citizen is revealed, once more, as the privileged white male. All others are defined in terms of their "difference" from this standard. Treating these others "equally" under the law perpetuates their inequality.

Feminist legal theorists have been on the forefront of exposing the partiality of this uniform standard and exploring what would be entailed by legal theory and practice without such a standard. It would be unfair to say, however, that all feminist legal theorists have jettisoned the concept of a monolithic legal subject and embraced multiplicity. Some have continued to argue for a neutral standard. But other feminist legal theorists have argued strongly that the monolithic standard informing our legal system is thoroughly masculine. The legal standard by which all cases are adjudicated is abstract and autonomous, that is, masculine. That which is specifically excluded from legal consideration is the relational, connected, and particular, that is, the feminine.

One of the most significant influences in feminist legal theory in the past several decades has been the attempt to integrate Gilligan's "care voice" into legal deliberations.[13] The relational subject theorized by Gilligan and other feminist theorists is the antithesis of the abstract universalism of the masculine/modernist subject. Thus bringing this voice into legal discussions profoundly alters these discussions. It replaces the abstract with the concrete and introduces a new form of legal reasoning specifically excluded by the justice voice, a relational, plural approach.

The most prominent advocate of the relational approach entailed by the care voice in legal discussions is Martha Minow. In *Making All the Difference: Inclusion, Exclusion, and American Law* (1990) Minow argues that we should shift the legal paradigm we use to conceive of difference from a focus on the distinctions between people to a focus on relationships within which we notice and draw distinctions (15). Minow attacks the central presupposition of our legal system's approach to difference—that there is an objective, neutral standard of normality from which differences can be assessed. Against this Minow argues, first, that no differences are pregiven, that all are embedded in social relationships, and, second, that the allegedly neutral, normal standard of the status quo is biased in favor of white males. She makes it clear that what she calls her "social-relations approach" amounts to a "profound challenge to conventional legal understandings" (217), that it may "threaten the very idea of law as authoritative and commanding" (224).

Other feminist legal theorists have also attempted to reveal the masculinity of the allegedly universal standard and what that entails for our legal sys-

---

13. See my *The Future of Differences* (1999) for a fuller discussion of this issue.

tem. Mary Frug, for example, explores how legal rules encode the female body with meaning and, specifically, encode it as different. Frug argues that legal discourse explains and rationalizes the meaning of the female body by appealing to "natural" sexual differences. The formal nature of legal neutrality, she asserts, conceals the way in which legal rules participate in the constitution of those meanings (1995, 495). She gives numerous examples of how legal discourse constructs women as the object of abuse, as mothers, and as sexual objects. This discourse, she asserts, constructs women as different from the neutral male standard. It is only in contrast to this neutral standard that women are different and thus subject to different legal treatment.

Zillah Eisenstein (1988) takes this argument one step further by arguing that the sex equality guaranteed by our legal system is illusory. Sex equality under the law means treating women like men. The law has no way of viewing the specificity of either the male sex/body *or* the female sex/body. As a way of challenging this, Eisenstein proposes introducing the pregnant body into the law in order to decenter the privileged position of the male body. Eisenstein's strategy reveals the failure of sex equality as it is presently conceived: the pregnant body cannot be treated equally to the male body because men cannot be pregnant. It thus poses an insoluble dilemma for legal equality.

In an argument that closely parallels that of Pateman, Eisenstein asserts that the legal notion of sex equality rests on the assertion that men and women are the same, but that the standard of sameness is that of the male (43). Much of Eisenstein's book is taken up with detailing how the legal discourse of sex equality is played out in the law and, specifically, how it disadvantages women. But there is another theme as well: exploring the radical implications of jettisoning the masculine standard. At the outset Eisenstein asserts that "my refocusing, therefore, does not establish a new homogeneous standard but rather denies the validity of having one at all" (2). Eisenstein's strategy of focusing on the pregnant body encourages us to recognize the particularities of the human body and to construct a notion of diversity that is compatible with equality (4). Her goal is what she calls "radical pluralism," a standard to replace the "abstract individualism of the male body and/or the father as the common denominator of what it means to be equal" (198). She concludes: "A feminism rooted in radical pluralism aims to destroy the hierarchy and the oppositions hierarchy constructs, and it seeks to create a view that recognizes a multiplicity of individuals who are free to be equal and equal in their freedom" (222).

Eisenstein's radical pluralism is indeed radical. Rejecting the monolithic masculine standard and replacing it with radical pluralism would quite literally transform our legal system. But exactly how it would transform it remains unclear in Eisenstein's work. Her references to radical pluralism are few and undeveloped. The key question, What would a legal system look like that did not have a monolithic standard? remains unanswered. Perhaps it is unfair to ask Eisenstein to provide such a vision. But I think it is significant that she has failed to do so. A picture, deeply embedded in our language and practice, is holding us captive here. It is almost impossible for us to imagine a legal system without a monolithic standard. It is almost impossible not to come to the conclusion that such a legal system would entail chaos. How would we know which of many standards to apply in any given case? Equally disturbing is the prospect of imagining a legal system in which specificity and particularity were at the center of legal discourse.

These difficulties are graphically illustrated in the dispute over the "reasonable woman" standard in recent legal theory and practice. The arguments both for and against reasonable woman highlight the issues of objectivity and embodiment that feminist legal theorists have raised. The impetus for employing a reasonable woman standard is the practical expression of the theoretical discussions of Minow, Frug, Eisenstein, and others. Particularly in cases involving rape, sexual harassment, and domestic violence it became clear, first, that the standard employed in these cases was a masculine standard and, second, that employing this standard produced outcomes that did not accord with women's experiences. In these instances if the same event were analyzed from a masculine and a feminine perspective, radically different evaluations of that event would follow. Thus, while a man would find an office pass pleasurable, a woman would experience it as harassment. While a man would find pornography enjoyable, a woman would find it objectifying. The legal result of these differences is that what women experience as injuries are not recognized or compensated as injuries if a masculine standard is applied (West 1991, 115–16).

The obvious remedy for this situation, at least from one perspective, is to apply a reasonable woman rather than a reasonable man standard in cases of rape, sexual harassment, and domestic violence. The first reference to the reasonable woman standard appeared in a dissent by Judge Damon Keith (significantly, an African American judge) in 1986. In their book on the reasonable woman standard, Caroline Forell and Donna Matthews declare that during the past twenty-five years, "most courts have replaced the reasonable man standard with that of the reasonable person" (2000, 6). And, in an increasing number of cases related to sexual matters, the reasonable person is in actuality a reasonable woman. The pivotal case establishing the reasonable woman standard was *Harris vs. Forklift Industries, Inc.* in 1993. In this case the reasonable woman standard was the sole criterion of whether the working environment in question was abusive (Forell 1994, 771).

In *A Law of Her Own: The Reasonable Woman as a Measure of Man* (2000)

Forell and Matthews make an impassioned argument for adopting a reasonable woman standard in cases of rape, sexual harassment, and domestic violence. In these cases, they argue, men's and women's life experiences and views of sex differ significantly and women are overwhelmingly the injured party (xvii). The key to their argument is the claim that when men *or women* sexually harass others they take on a stereotypically masculine role that derives pleasure from dominating others. In contrast the authors state that "[t]he reasonable woman standard respects other workers' bodily integrity, agency, and personal autonomy and expects the same in return" (71). Courts that use a reasonable woman standard, they argue, "dramatically depart from the traditional judicial posture of 'neutrality' and acknowledge that the law contains male biases" (17).

The issue of neutrality as it relates to the reasonable woman standard, however, is more complex than Forell and Matthews acknowledge in this passage. It is true, as they assert, that the reasonable woman standard reveals the masculine bias of the law. But it is also clear that the defenders of the reasonable woman standard do not want to jettison objectivity and neutrality in the law altogether. They only want to reveal a specifically masculine bias and replace it. They do not, in other words, embrace Eisenstein's radical pluralism. What Forell and Matthews argue for is *another* objective standard, reasonable woman, that would apply in the three categories of legal cases they discuss. Their argument is that the reasonable woman standard is a more appropriate objective standard in these cases. It represents values that transcend a particular class or race, and even, they assert, gender (19).

Forell and Matthews's defense of the reasonable woman standard, then, rests on the claim to objectivity and a rejection of what they call "subjectivity." The reasonable woman standard has been criticized as essentializing "woman." Forell and Matthews's reply is that the reasonable woman standard does not force women to deny other aspects of their identity (84). The authors concede that issues other than sexism, most notably racism, are frequently factors particularly in cases of sexual harassment. They further note that some courts have routinely incorporated factors other than gender, usually race and sexual orientation, into the sexual harassment decision (86). But the authors see a danger in this strategy. They argue that "problems frequently occur" in such combined claims. Consequently, the claimant in sexual harassment cases should have a choice whether to bring a combined claim (89).

Forell and Matthers's worries about complicating the reasonable woman standard with other factors are not unfounded. They note that the Equal Employment Opportunities Commission's guidelines, which were never promulgated, provided that the reasonable person standard includes race, color, religion, gender, age, disability, religion, and national origin. A few courts, furthermore, have adopted such multifaceted standards. One federal court (the nineteenth) has established a "reasonable woman of color" standard (Forell and Matters 2000, 92). Forell and Matthews are opposed to this move toward multiple standards. They assert: "If all the many aspects of a person's social identity were considered in assessing harassment claims where sexualization or sexism were the core harm involved, standards would virtually disappear in the subjective nature of the inquiry" (94).

As Forell and Matthews's defense of the reasonable woman standard indicates, however, there is another side to this issue. Feminist critics of the reasonable woman standard counter that, despite the protests of its defenders, the standard is essentializing. It presumes that all women would judge experience from the same perspective. They further assert that the reasonable woman standard is objectionable on epistemological grounds. It is, like the reasonable man standard, an explicitly objective standard that conforms to the epistemology of law in a liberal society. It presupposes that we need a universal, or quasi-universal, standard for that law to operate. Even more pointedly, there is the notion of reasonable itself. Reason is a masculine trait. *Reasonable woman* is in some sense an oxymoron. Reason is what liberal law is all about. Thus, the reasonable woman standard, far from challenging that law, conforms to it (Wildman 2000; Cahn 1992).

From the perspective I am developing here, however, the most significant aspect of this debate is the discussion of multifaceted standards of judgment and the danger of "subjectivity." Commenting on Title VII legislation, one judge remarked that extending the categories in this legislation turns the question of employment discrimination into a "many-headed Hydra." Protected subgroups would exist for every possible combination of race, color, sex, national origin, and religion (Abrams 1994, 2496–97). This "many-headed Hydra" is the radical pluralism that Eisenstein advocates. It is the subjective standard that Forell and Matthews fear. Reasonable woman is, indeed, a move away from the monolithic masculine standard of the law. But the discussion of this concept makes it clear that moving further away, into what Kathryn Abrams (1994) calls a "complex female subject," seems to scare almost everyone. The idea that each case would be decided on the "subjective" perception of the woman involved is not a viable option for most theorists and legal actors.

My point in reviewing the work of these feminist legal theorists is to argue that their work is an important step in the direction of imagining a polity of embodied citizens. Introducing the specificity of the male and female bodies into legal discourse is a radical step. It challenges the impartiality of the universal standard and moves toward a system in which difference and diversity are central. This discussion also reveals the deeply rooted resistance to such a step. Another group of legal theorists have also been exploring this territory: critical race theorists. Like the feminist legal theorists cited above, critical race theorists are concerned both to reveal the partiality of our legal standard and to suggest a legal system that focuses on rather than eschews difference.

Critical race theory, an offshoot of critical legal theory, addresses the problems created by the historical presence of racism in our society. There are two principal trajectories of this movement. The first is the argument that the problem of racism in our society is a cultural and not a legal problem. Discrimination against nonwhites is deeply rooted in our culture and is not subject to purely legal remedy. Critical race theorists see law as a cultural product, not as a separate entity. By defining racism as a cultural phenomenon, they argue both that the law is complicit in perpetuating racism and that eradicating racism is more than a legal problem. As one proponent of critical race theory puts it, "Critical Race Theory can mature toward a significant representation of cultural analysis as it bears on legal values and thereby move to destroy the foundations and structures of racial subordination" (Calmore 1995, 324).

The second trajectory of critical race theory is closely related: challenging the ahistoricism and objectivity of the law. Mari Matsuda, for example, argues that critical race theory always sees law in context and thus expresses skepticism toward the dominant legal claims of neutrality, objectivity, color blindness, and meritocracy (Matsuda et al. 1993, 6). Critical race theory, like certain aspects of feminist legal theory, sees the law not as removed from social practice, but as a system of meanings that construct social reality (Iglesias 1997, 329). Our ideology defines law as rational, abstract, and principled. Critical race theory challenges this both by challenging the privileging of these qualities over their opposites, the concrete and contextual, and by challenging whether in fact the law lives up to this ideal. Law, they argue, is a form of human activity, not the transcendent arbiter of that activity (Olsen 1995).

It is significant that both the feminist legal theorists I have cited and critical race theorists are on the margins of legal theory and practice; they provide a radical alternative to dominant legal thinking. Both approaches are radical in the literal meaning of the word: they attack the root of our legal system. Their challenge has two elements. First, they challenge whether the objective, universal standard informing our legal system is, in fact, neutral. They argue that the alleged neutrality of that standard masks the white, male body, the abstract citizen that informs liberalism itself. Second, most of these theorists challenge whether we need a neutral standard at all. They point to the embeddedness of law in our culture, how it structures meanings and social practices. They suggest, although only tentatively, that a neutral standard is both impossible and undesirable. They suggest that in a society structured by race and gender we need a legal system that takes account of this, not one that ignores it.

At this point it might seem obvious to argue that, in recent years, there has been a very prominent movement to do precisely what these theorists are advocating: bringing race and gender into legal deliberations. Affirmative action legislation seems to move our legal system away from a universal standard and toward the embodiment and particularity for which these theorists are arguing. But if we look carefully at affirmative action legislation, exactly the opposite conclusion emerges. This legislation does, indeed, bring race and gender into the law, particularities that, according to our legal ideology, have no place in adjudication. But an examination of the history and practice of this legislation reveals that it affirms rather than challenges the ideology of the neutrality of law. First, the extensive and ongoing resistance to this legislation indicates how deeply rooted the ideology of neutrality is in our legal and social system. The idea that race and gender have legal status is repugnant to that ideology. The checkered history of affirmative action legislation is testimony to that fact. It is continually and successfully challenged on grounds that affirm the ideology of neutrality.

The second respect in which this legislation affirms our legal ideology is the basic assumption on which it rests: it is a temporary measure. Affirmative action legislation could only be justified by presenting it as an unfortunate and temporary intrusion into an otherwise neutral legal system. This legislation was not justified by arguments that revealed the nonneutrality of our legal system. Nor was it buttressed by arguments for jettisoning that neutrality altogether. Rather, affirmative action legislation was justified only as a measure that was, unfortunately, necessary at this historical juncture. It was designed to be temporary, not permanent. The clear assumption behind this legislation is that the neutral standard that informs the legal system will be reinstated after this brief experiment in difference. Not even the proponents of this legislation argue that there was no neutral standard to return *to*. Matsuda comments:

> The very controversy reveals how deeply they cut into the unresolved dilemma of neutrality that lies at the heart of American law. These proposals add up to a new jurisprudence, one founded not on an ideal of neutrality but on the reality of oppression. These proposals recognize that this has always been a nation of dominate and dominated and that changing that pattern will require affirmative, non-neutral measures designed to make the least the most and to bring peace, at last, to this land. (Matsuda 1996, 10)

Conclusion

> Uncle Theo fingered the mauve and white pebbles on the
> beach. These stones, which brought such pleasure to the twins,
> were a nightmare to Theo. Their multiplicity and randomness
> appalled him.... The pebbles ... looked at closely ... exhib-
> ited every indeterminate color and also varied considerably in
> size and shape. All were rounded, but some were flattish, some
> oblong, some spherical; some were almost transparent, others
> more or less capriciously speckled, others close-textured and
> nearly black, a few of a brownish-red, some of a pale grey,
> others of a purple that was almost blue.
>
> —Iris Murdoch *The Nice and the Good*

Elizabeth Spelman quotes this passage from Iris Murdoch's novel *The Nice and the Good* in her *Inessential Woman*. Spelman's point is that Western thought in general and feminist thought in particular share an important trait with Uncle Theo: a fear of multiplicity. Since Plato and Aristotle, thinkers in the Western tradition have attempted to subsume heterogeneity under general concepts. Undifferentiated multiplicity makes us nervous. We want to organize and control it by generalizing the multiplicity. Wittgenstein puts this nicely when he argues that the "illness" of philosophy is, above all else, a "craving for generality" (1960, 17). Spelman's thesis is that this tendency is pernicious. It obscures heterogeneity and creates hierarchy. Through the establishment of a generic definition, all the cases that fall under that definition are ranked in terms of the degree to which they conform to it. Few cases measure up to the ideal defined by the concept; most are ranked as inferior.

Spelman's goal is to challenge this tendency in feminist theory. She wants to jettison the concept "woman" because it establishes the dominance of the white, middle-class heterosexual woman. Because feminism has defined "woman" in these terms, all women who deviate from this definition fall under the category of "other." The result is that the differences between women are obscured and a hierarchy of differences is created. Spelman's counter to this is that we should focus on differences rather than ignore them. Conscious that she is flaunting a deeply ingrained tendency, she nevertheless asserts that this is the direction that feminism should take: "Finally, given our discussion above of the perils of trying to 'transcend' differences, can we confidently affirm that it is any less politically dangerous *not* to focus on them? For whom is it less politically dangerous? Will 'not focusing' on differences among women guarantee that no woman's concerns will take priority over another's?" (1988, 15).

There is an obvious parallel between Spelman's argument and that which I have advanced in this chapter. Spelman argues that there is no generic woman, Pateman and others that there is no generic citizen. Spelman argues that the generic concept "woman" obscures differences and creates hierarchy. Pateman's analysis leads to the same conclusion with regard to the generic "citizen." Spelman argues that we should take the risk of focusing on difference rather commonality, creating a feminist politics that eschews generic woman. I am arguing the same for politics as a whole. The reign of the generic citizen has produced the "others" who are excluded from full participation in politics because they do not match the definition of "citizen." But because this definition is not acknowledged, the veiled citizen of the liberal polity and the allegedly neutral standard of our legal system have not been challenged. Instead of transforming liberalism, identity politics has reinforced the hierarchy implicit in it.

Why not, then, jettison the generic citizen? Why not focus on differences rather than uniformity? There are several obvious objections to this strategy. The first is the subject of Tully's analysis of constitutionalism: a picture holds us captive. Since the rise of liberal constitutionalism, difference has been defined as discrimination, uniformity as justice. Liberalism represents a rejection of the reign of status, the traditional organization of society by status hierarchy rather than by individual merit. To focus on difference at the expense of neutrality/objectivity is to risk the return of discrimination. Once we allow differences back in, the discrimination that marked the past seems an inevitable consequence.

A second objection is that without a uniform standard we invite chaos. A uniform standard allows us to judge everyone by the same standards and, thus, justly. If we apply different standards in different cases we will be unable to insure that all citizens are treated fairly. We will also have the problem of deciding which standards to use in which cases. How will we decide what criteria to use in each case if we do not have a single standard that applies to all cases?

Meeting these objections is difficult. Tully is right: the picture that holds us captive here is powerful. If we add Spelman's perspective to this picture it takes on even more force. Tully paints the picture in political terms. Spelman defines it philosophically and identifies it as endemic to Western thought. But, like Spelman, I want to argue that we should take the risk of difference. My principal argument in defense of this risk is that difference has never been obliterated, it has only been veiled. The neutral citizen/legal standard was and is a fiction that hides the reign of the dominant white male elite. We have never had a neutral standard; we do not have one to return to. The picture is distorted. The generic citizen is just as different as the rest of us.[14]

In her argument for taking the risk of difference, Spelman argues, "Spotting differences among women is no more likely to involve making invidious distinctions among us than refusing to note differences" (1988, 175). Let's look at what happens when we apply this argument to citizens. Applying the same standard to all citizens has both produced and perpetuated inequality. What if we jettison uniformity and attempt to adjudicate cases on the basis of the standards appropriate to each particular case? Eisenstein gives an example of what this would entail in her discussion of pregnant women. There is no universal standard by which the case of the pregnant woman can be adjudicated. The only appropriate standard is the welfare of a particular woman in a particular situation. She must be treated as a unique case, not as the instantiation of a uniform standard.

Affirmative action legislation provides another example. Critical race theorists argue that the law is not above society, but is both produced by and produces social reality. The historical legacy of racism dictates the need for the special treatment of African Americans. Treating them equally before the law perpetuates the inequality created by that historical legacy. But it does not follow from this that every disadvantaged group in society should be judged by the same standard. Other groups have suffered discrimination. Asian Americans and Hispanics, like African Americans, have been denied full citizenship. Yet the historical legacy of each is unique. Each dictates a unique approach, a standard appropriate to their particular case.

Take the case of the Amish. In a strictly material sense, the Amish have less of the things that many Americans want. The Amish way of life emphasizes obedience, conformity, patriarchy, and hierarchy, values that many Americans would contest. Furthermore, the Amish do not encourage their children to think critically about that way of life. Despite this, in 1972 the U.S. Supreme Court ruled in *Wisconsin vs. Yoder* that the Amish had the right to keep their children out of the local public high school. The majority opinion in this case contained a long discussion of the Amish way of life that indicated an obvious

14. In *Moral Understandings* (1998), Margaret Urban Walker argues against what she calls the "theoretical-juridical model" of moral theory that defines morality as a set of lawlike propositions that "the" moral agent must conform to. Like Spelman and Pateman, Walker argues that we need a more contextualized, specific approach.

admiration for it. Although the court recognized that Amish children would be disadvantaged as adults if they were to leave the Amish community, they nevertheless upheld the community's right to educate those children.[15]

My point is not that the Court's ruling was wrong or right. Rather, it is that the Amish case cannot be adjudicated by appeal to a uniform standard that subsumes all "disadvantaged" groups. As Joseph Carens notes in his discussion of the Amish, the connection between inequality and culture is different in the black and Amish cases (2000, 98). The disadvantage of the Amish is of a very different nature than that of African Americans or, for that matter, any other group. The situation and claims of each group require a legal perspective that recognizes that uniqueness.

The radical pluralism I am advocating here constitutes a sea change in our political/legal conceptions. This is largely a result of the understanding of identity that informs this conception. The relational, situated self defined by object relations theory entails a politics rooted in difference, not uniformity. It is not my goal here to outline the practical implications of such a change. But, on the theoretical level, I want to suggest what may appear to be two contradictory theses. First, I am arguing that only a radical transformation of our political/legal system can meet the challenge of identity. Identity politics and multiculturalism have pushed us to the point where many are beginning to question the viability of a uniform standard. Even the conservative jurist Richard Posner has argued that the differences in our society are irreconcilable and that we must make some provision in the law to accommodate these differences. His suggestion is that we appoint judges who represent the different groups in order that the differences be fairly heard. I do not endorse this solution, but its premise is much the same as that for which I am arguing. Accommodating difference demands multiplicity, not uniformity. And multiplicity changes everything.

My second thesis is that despite the radical change entailed by jettisoning uniformity, aspects of our legal/political system can and are beginning to move in that direction. The Amish are treated as a unique group, not subsumed under a uniform standard. The concepts of "reasonable woman" and even "reasonable woman of color" are making headway in legal discussions. I will elaborate on this argument in Chapter 4. At this point I want to suggest that there is evidence that our system is beginning to accommodate difference despite itself.

---

15. I am relying here on Joseph Carens's (2000) discussion of the Amish.

3

Identity Politics—the Personal and the Political

Identity Politics: The Critiques

In the previous chapter I argued that identity politics violates the basic tenets of the liberal polity. It brings identity into the public sphere, challenging the liberal injunction against mixing the particular and the universal. It tears the veil from the abstract, neutral citizen of liberalism, reveals his identity, and moves in the direction of an embodied rather than a universal citizen. It deconstructs the neat public/private distinction at the heart of liberalism by suggesting a broader conception of power that shapes identities. But I also argued that this analysis of the politics of identity is incomplete. It does not address two key issues: the relationship between individual and group identity and the definition of a broader conception of power that goes beyond politics. These problems are the subject of this and the following chapter.

There is another sense in which my argument is incomplete: I have not addressed the critiques and defenses of identity politics that have been advanced in recent years. The recent critiques of identity politics have called into question the fundamental assumptions of this politics. These critiques, furthermore, cannot be dismissed by employing the argument I developed earlier. The problems with identity politics that they reveal are not entirely a product of the constraints that the liberal polity places on identity politics. On the contrary, the analyses developed in these critiques question whether identity politics is viable as a basis for politics under any conditions. Unless these critiques are addressed, any argument for identity politics cannot stand. Few of the defenses of identity politics, furthermore, meet the issues raised in these critiques directly. Relying on these defenses alone will not suffice for developing an argument for the practice.

It is tempting to divide the critiques of identity politics into two broad categories: internal and external. Some critiques focus on the effect of identity politics on individual identity. These critiques argue that identity politics necessarily erases difference and enforces uniformity. Other critiques focus on the strictly political effects of identity politics. They question the political implications of introducing groups into the political and legal arena, thereby extending state power over these groups. But although this division seems obvious in many ways, it is a false dichotomy. It is impossible, where identity is concerned, to separate the internal and the external, the individual and the political. The two aspects of identity are in constant interaction. Individual identity informs political identity and vice versa. Although distinguishable, the two cannot be neatly divided.

The most obvious criticism of identity politics is one that is implicit in the defenses of liberalism that were discussed in the preceding chapter. From the perspective of liberalism, identity politics threatens the very possibility of politics because it celebrates personal identity over the identity of the universal citizen. In Sheldon Wolin's words, the politics of difference has rendered suspect the language and possibility of collectivity, common action, and shared purpose (1993, 480). Jean Bethke Elshtain has been particularly vehement in advancing this critique of identity politics. The citizen, she claims, "gives way before the aggrieved member of a self-defined or contained group" (1995, 53). The claim of difference, she asserts, "tells me nothing that is civically interesting" (67). The result of the politics of difference and the "retribalization" it entails, Elshtain concludes, is the demise of democracy itself (74).

Elshtain's criticism is rooted in a basic assumption that informs the liberal polity: without the separation between public and private, political action is impossible. But critics such as Elshtain make no attempt to defend this assumption. The dichotomy between the private and public spheres defines politics in the liberal polity, but why must we assume that it defines politics per se? Why is it the case that removing the public/private distinction removes the possibility of collective political action? Why is political action impossible for the embodied citizens of identity politics? In what sense does bringing the particularities of identity into the political sphere make it impossible for citizens to unite around a political goal? Given the problems incurred by the universal citizen of liberalism, it is incumbent on the critics of identity politics to defend this assumption. Merely asserting that this is impossible does more to reveal the liabilities of liberalism than to show the impossibility of identity politics.

This criticism of identity politics, however, is not at the forefront of the debate that the practice has engendered. The central criticism of identity politics is one that, particularly in the feminist community, has its roots in Judith Butler's theory of the subject: the claim that it entails the fixing of identity. It is significant that Elshtain refers to this critique in her attack on identity politics. Advocates of the politics of difference, Elshtain declares, advocate their own version of sameness—exclusionist sameness along the lines of gender, race, ethnicity, and sexual preference (75). The criticism that identity politics does not avoid the fixing of identity that characterizes the liberal polity but merely fixes identity in a new location is a pervasive theme in discussions of identity politics. In the feminist community and beyond, this critique has been influential in calling into question the viability of the practice. More than any other argument it has been influential in turning feminists and others away from identity politics.

The definitive statement of this critique within feminism is Butler's discussion in *Gender Trouble*. This work is, in some sense, an extended polemic against the possibility of an identity politics rooted in the identity of "woman." Butler's central argument is that embracing the identity "woman" places feminism in the modernist camp. Her claim is that the identity of "woman" is just as foundational as the modernist subject it seeks to replace and thus must be avoided as a feminist political strategy. To many feminists, Butler's critique, like the theory of identity that informs it, has been decisive. Admonitions against reifying identity or assuming the existence of an essential identity are everywhere in the feminist literature. It would be difficult today to find a feminist who would defend an essential identity for "woman" or any of the other identities that inform feminist identity politics: "lesbian," "Chicana," "woman of color," and so on.

Shane Phelan's analysis of the detrimental effect of fixing identity within the lesbian community highlights the essential elements of this critique. In *Identity Politics* (1989) Phelan argues, "What has been accepted in the lesbian community is not the lesbian, but the *Lesbian*—the politically/sexually/culturally correct being, the carrier of *the* lesbian feminist consciousness" (57). Because of the perceived need to impose unity in the lesbian community, this singular definition has come to be imposed on all lesbians. As a result, Phelan argues, communities defined as lesbian fail to give individuals room to develop as unique, conflict-ridden individuals (78). In an argument that parallels that of Spelman, Phelan asserts that we must focus on differences as well as commonalities; the need for unity does not entail the need for homogeneity (159–65). She concludes: "Identity politics must be based not only on identity, but on the appreciation of politics as the art of living together. Politics that ignores our identities, that makes them 'private' is useless, but non-negotiable identities will enslave us whether they are imposed from within or without" (170).

In her following book, *Getting Specific: Postmodern Lesbian Politics* (1994), Phelan elaborates on these theses. Here she advocates what she calls a "politics of specificity," which forces us to think about difference contextually, not abstractly (9). She asserts that lesbians should enter politics as people occupying a "provisional subject position," in other words, she advocates a nonidentity politics. What results is a coalition politics that focuses not on what we share but on what we *might* share as we develop our identities through the process of coalition (140). This constitutes a departure from her previous book. There Phelan argued for the retention of identity politics but one in which we carefully distinguish between the sorts of identity issues that are vital to our growth and freedom and those that are not (1989, 133). Here she has abandoned even that tenuous connection to identity.

The question of the fixing of identity that occurs in identity politics is of paramount importance. Those who condemn this tendency are expressing a legitimate concern. Butler, Phelan, and the other critics of identity politics are right: moving from the fixed identity of liberalism/modernism to the multiple identities of identity politics is not the solution to the problems created by the politics of modernism. In both cases, differences are occluded and hierarchies established and maintained. Although the concept "woman" moves us away from the masculine "citizen" it does not move far enough. It still partakes of the essentialism of modernist identity that was the problem in the first place.

But although the danger that these critiques have revealed is a legitimate one, the critiques are nevertheless flawed in several crucial respects. First, Butler and those who adopt her position claim that the assertion of any stable identity is equivalent to a return to modernism and the essential subject. But, as I argued in Chapter 1, this is not the case. The object relations theorists have shown that some concept of a stable identity is necessary to psychic health. They have also shown that this identity is socially constructed, not essential. It follows that we are not forced to choose between Butler's fictive subject or even Phelan's "provisional subject position" and the modernist essentialist subject. Instead we can and must assert a subject with a constructed, yet stable, identity. Unless we do so we cannot posit the subject as a political actor. Butler's fictive self cannot operate in the political arena or anywhere else.

The second problem with this critique is that it fails to examine the relationship between personal identity and the "identity" of identity politics. Butler's theory obviates the possibility of talking about personal identity. Those who adopt her theory presume that any discussion of personal identity is inherently modernist and therefore suspect. But an understanding of identity politics necessitates distinguishing between the "identity" of politics and personal identity. If the "identity" of identity politics is not the same as the personal identity of the participants of that politics, then the fixing of identity is no longer a problem. If we imagine an identity politics that is an interface between personal and public identities, then we can sidestep the problems posed by this critique of the practice. In order to accomplish this, however, we need to do some difficult theoretical work on identity. These critiques fail to provide that work.

Implicit in this discussion is another issue that Phelan touches on but does not develop. She argues that every new definition of identity is a choice with political consequences, an investiture of meaning, a process of location (1989, 78–79). Her redefinition of identity politics involves distinguishing different sorts of identity issues and deciding which are important, which are trivial. What Phelan is talking about here is power. What I am calling public identities are about power. They are social constructions that define the public identities that structure our social world (Scott 1995, 6). We can accept them, resist them, redefine them, but they are nevertheless constitutive of our identities. Understanding identity politics necessarily entails understanding how this power operates.

Although discussions of power are not absent from the literature on identity politics, I am arguing that power should be a more central emphasis of those analyses. Looking at Phelan's "Lesbian" provides an example of what I mean by looking at identity politics from the perspective of power. Before the advent of identity politics, "lesbian" was a public identity that was defined as degraded, debased, even sick. To be labeled a lesbian was to be vilified, excluded from acceptable human society, reviled. For obvious reasons, few lesbians identified with this public identity. The rise of what Phelan calls the "Lesbian" is an attempt to redefine this public category. It is an attempt to challenge the hegemonic power in society that categorizes lesbians as immoral and reprehensible. The "Lesbian" is a positive category. It defines women with a sexual orientation to other women as powerful and proud. As such, it is a public identity that women can affirm. To identify as a "Lesbian" is to at once challenge the power that defined "lesbian" as debased and positively to affirm one's sexual orientation.

What is *not* going on in this process, however, is an abandonment of one's personal identity. Here Phelan is wrong. Lesbians are not adopting a "provisional subject position" when they engage in political activity. Rather, they are identifying with a redefined public category for political purposes. Although they make that identification from the perspective of their personal identities, those personal identities are not obliterated by the public identity. Furthermore, unless each lesbian possessed a personal identity, she would be unable to make the identification that makes possible her participation in identity politics.

A corollary of the problem of fixing identity is the issue of multiple identities. Phelan refers to this problem when she argues that the diversity of lesbians' lives is lost when subsumed under the "Lesbian." Personal identities are composed of multiple elements. From the perspective of public identity categories, those elements may be contradictory. Identifying with only one public identity category can seem to some women to be a denial of the other aspects of their identity. The problem of multiple aspects of identity is frequently raised in the writings of third-wave feminists. Anthologies of third-wave feminists frequently focus on diversity, highlighting the multiplicity of women's identities and lifestyles. The author of one of these accounts, Sonja Curry-Johnson, confesses to an "acute sense of multiplicity" (1995, 222). The multiple identities that she feels define her also divide her. "Each identity defines me; each is responsible for elements of my character; from each I devise some sustenance for my soul." But these identities do not peacefully coexist. The effort to blend them together harmoniously she describes as "desperate." Curry-Johnson's article is, in some sense, a cry for help. She feels that women should be able to "bring our full selves to the table." But she also does not see how this could be made possible.

This sense of multiplicity is made even more acute if one of the identities in the mix is a marginalized racial identity. In the era of identity politics, many women feel they have to choose between an identity as "woman" or "African American," "Chicana," and so on. The politics of each of these identity groups is exclusive. It demands a singular allegiance to the identity category that defines it and the political goals it has articulated. The result, for women who are forced to navigate these political demands, is a sense of fragmentation. Lourdes Torres, for example, argues that many Latina authors experience a fragmented identity, an inability to speak from a "unified, non-contradictory subject position" (1991, 275). María Lugones takes this argument a step further by arguing that the unity of identity is a privilege accorded only those who belong to the dominant culture (1987). Those who do not, those who must juggle the identities of woman, Latina, lesbian, and so forth, must "travel" from one identity to another. This travel, Lugones argues, may not be willful or even conscious. "Rather one is someone who has that personality or character or uses space and language in a particular way. The 'one' here does not refer to some underlying 'I.' One does not *experience* any underlying 'I'" (1987, 11–12).

The position Lugones is adopting here is informed by the Butleresque definition of identity that I am challenging. Against Lugones and Butler I am asserting that there *is* an "I" who experiences these identities, that travels from one to another. This "I" is constituted by the childhood experiences of the individual who is subsumed under these categories. Although the construction of personal identity is profoundly affected by public identity categories, children are typically not aware of this. Rather, when they become adolescents and adults, they gradually become aware of the existence of public identity categories and begin to realize that they are subsumed under these public categories. One is classified as a lesbian, a woman, a Chicana, a political activist, a professor, and a whole host of other categories. One also becomes aware that these public categories impinge on one's life, creating in many cases contradictions or confusions. But much of the confusion stems from ignoring the difference between public and personal identity. Public identity categories define all of us and demean some of us. They define elements of our personal identities as contradictory. The contradiction stems from the public categories, not personal identity. What identity politics is all about is contesting the power of those public categories and the definitions they foster. What I am suggesting is that if we conceptualize identity politics in terms of power—challenging the power of public categories to define us and choosing to identify with a different public identity—then we can better understand the "traveling" that Lugones describes.[1]

A critic of identity politics who focuses on the issue of power is Wendy Brown. In *States of Injury: Power and Freedom in Late Modernity* (1995) Brown indicts identity politics as a contemporary version of Nietzsche's politics of *ressentiment*. She defines identity politics as the tendency to pursue legal redress for injuries related to social subordination by marked attributes—race, sexuality, and so forth. This practice, she claims, fixes the identity of the injured as social position. Law then becomes a neutral arbiter of injury, the legitimate protection against injury (27). Those who engage in identity politics

---

1. Torres makes a similar point when she argues that a politics of activism is a politics that seeks to recognize, name, and destroy the system of domination that subjugates people of color (1991, 275). See also Ortega 2001.

to right historic political injustices are forced by the logic of that politics to embrace an identity that, if the politics is successful, is fixed in legal codes.

In developing her argument, Brown relies on many of the tenets of Butler's theory of identity. She sees identity politics as a reaction against postmodernity's deconstruction of collective identity. The new feminist politics that she calls for is one that loosens attachments to subjectivity, identity, and morality (Brown 1995, 51). Like Butler she argues that resistance cannot be effective if it partakes in any way of hegemonic power. Thus identity politics structured by resentment is invested in its own subjection, its own impotence. In its emergence as a protest against marginalization or subordination, politicized identity becomes attached to its own exclusion. She concludes that these politicized identities have no future; they cannot triumph over the pain that they embrace (70–74).

Brown also follows Butler in adopting an either/or stance toward identity and power. Since stable identity is the hallmark of modernism, it must be rejected. Since hegemonic power establishes and maintains these identities, it must be rejected as well. But Brown, like Butler, must then confront the difficult question of how this power can be resisted. She poses the question quite clearly: what kind of political recognition can identity-based claims seek that do not resubordinate the subject through categories that originated in an effort to subordinate these subjects? (55). But although Brown is very specific about the kinds of politics that do *not* achieve this goal, those that do remain vague. The structure of her argument constrains the possible answers she can advance. She cannot advocate a stable female identity as the basis for identity politics, because, as she asserts, female identity is irreconcilable with the "diverse and multiple vectors of power constructing and diversifying identity." But, she concludes, even though gender identities are impossible to generalize, gender *power* may be named and traced with some precision (1995, 166).

Brown is not the only theorist to advance this critique of identity politics.[2] The significant advantage of this position is that it focuses on power. It emphasizes that the public identities that demean and subordinate individuals are created and maintained by hegemonic power. It reveals that there are no essential identities, but instead, social constructions. Identity politics is an attempt to contest this power, to challenge both the definition of a particular identity and the power that enforces it. Brown and the other critics of identity politics who take this perspective, however, do not see it this way. They

2. See Scott 1995 and Aronowitz 1995. Using Hannah Arendt's work, Bonnie Honig (1992) develops a related argument by articulating a "performative politics" that transforms private identities.

argue that identity politics is complicit in the power that fixes identities as injured and thus cannot be transformative.

But this conclusion is not necessarily entailed by an analysis of the role of power in identity politics. The Brown/Butler position on this issue is elegant, simple, and wrong. Hegemonic power creates the reality in which we live. This reality is a social construct, not an essential, ontological fact. It follows that resisting that reality can *only* be done in the terms that that reality creates. Thus the strategy of resistance advocated by Brown that somehow (how?) transcends that reality cannot be effective precisely because it does not address that reality. For ontological reasons Brown wants to move out of the reality created by hegemonic power. But identity politics is about power, not ontology. Public identities are social constructions that constrain us, but they are not essential or universal. In fact, identity politics reveals the social construction of identities precisely by challenging those constructions. Because they are social constructions, they can be contested with other social constructions. When a lesbian contests "lesbian," the degenerate woman who loves other women, with "Lesbian," the proud lover of women, she is making a power move. She is fighting one social construction with another.

One of the key elements of Brown's critique of identity politics is that the success of identity politics has come to be defined in legal terms. The structure of identity politics dictates that it is successful when the group is legally recognized as a disadvantaged group, enabling it to seek legal redress. This can take the form of including the group on the census form, thus enabling the government to collect statistics on income, family makeup, and so on. Or it can take the form of judicial recognition as a protected group that is due special consideration under the law. Brown has two problems with this. First, it fixes the identity of the group *as* disadvantaged, as victims in need of state assistance. Second, it extends state power. The state is defined as the source of the redress of grievances. Although she does not elaborate on this point, it is clear what Brown means here. U.S. government policies have been the source of much of the discrimination and disadvantage suffered by groups such as women, African Americans, and Asians. To cast the government as the savior of these groups obscures this history and paints a false picture of the state's role in discrimination.

Brown's criticisms here are well taken. Legally fixing groups as disadvantaged should not be the goal of identity politics. There are serious political drawbacks to institutionalizing groups as disadvantaged. Brown mentions two of these drawbacks. Other critics of identity politics have pointed to others. Phelan discusses how the creation of the "Lesbian" erases differences between individual lesbians. Her concern is primarily the internal politics of the lesbian identity group. This erasure of difference, however, also has a negative effect in the external political arena. Entering the political arena as a particular identity group implies a unified public stance. A particular public perception of the identity group will inevitably emerge; all members of that groups will be assumed to conform to that public perception. This is a definition imposed from without, not from within. In many, probably most, cases it conflicts with the self-identification of the identity group.

The women's movement in the contemporary United States is a good example of this phenomenon. In the public eye, feminists are all the same. They hate men, greatly exaggerate the problems faced by women in this society, are at war with the traditional family, and are mostly lesbians. Furthermore, they always have a single stance on any given political issue. The media will report "the feminists' position" on a current issue without bothering to explore differences even between individual organized feminist groups. This public perception of "the feminist" has a pervasive effect on the feminist movement. It largely accounts for the low number of people, men or women, who define themselves as feminists. It erases differences between feminists and categorizes feminists who have important disagreements—for example, antipornography and anticensorship feminists—as the same.

The effect of this externally imposed unity is particularly pernicious in the case of panethnic identity groups in the contemporary United States. Scholars of social movements argue that the formation of a social/political group appears to grow from a combination of internal and external forces. The distinguishing feature of a social movement is the assertion of an identity in public life. A collective identity, from this perspective, is the shared definition of a group that derives from members' common interests, experiences, and solidarity. Thus the formation of a social movement appears to be very straightforward: individuals possess the same identity and as a result come together in a common social movement. But the reality is not so simple. Research has shown that individuals do not bring ready-made identities to collective action (Rupp and Taylor 1999, 365). Cultural differences, for example, are only potential identity markers for members of ethnic groups. This potential must be taken up and mobilized to create an ethnic group (Espiritu 1992, 9). It does not occur spontaneously.

In his discussion of the emergence of a panethnic movement for Asian Americans, Espiritu (1992) paints a picture in which forces in the external political/ social environment, not the perception of a shared identity, play the major role in the formation of the political movement. Espiritu argues that in the evolution of a panethnic group, identity emerges out of recognition of a common fate, a fate imposed by the dominant community. He argues, "When the state uses the ethnic label as a unit in economic allocations and political representations, ethnic groups find it both convenient and necessary to act collectively" (10). Panethnic movements call attention to the coercively imposed nature of ethnicity. Ethnicity is not a matter of choice. Rather, people are categorized into ethnic groups by those in power. The hegemonic group imposes a categorical identity on people that is defined as inherently different from and, by implication, inferior to the dominant group. Differences within the category are ignored by the dominant group. As a result, groups often join forces when they recognize that their differences have been ignored (3–7). Espiritu concludes, "[P]an-ethnic groups in the US are products of political and social processes rather than cultural bonds" (13).[3]

Espiritu's analysis puts the phenomenon of ethnic politics in the United States in a different light. Ethnic groups are, in theory, voluntary collectives defined by national origin whose members share a distinctive, integrated culture. In practice, however, ethnic politics in the United States is something quite different. Political necessity has thrown together ethnic groups who, at best, have little in common and, at worst, have a history of ethnic hatred. Groups categorized as, for example, "Asian" or "Hispanic" are made up of diverse peoples; their designation is a result of the dominant group's inability or unwillingness to recognize their differences. The "ethnic" movement that results is thus a product of the necessities of liberal politics and the legal categories created by that politics. It unites individuals with little or no "natural" ethnic similarities and forces them to ignore their differences for political and legal purposes. Such a politics emphasizes the constructed, political character of ethnic categories and the constitutive role of dominant institutions.

Identity Politics: The Defenses

These criticisms of identity politics cannot be dismissed lightly. They raise fundamental questions about the viability of any politics based on identity. Few of the critics of identity politics, however, argue that we should abandon identity altogether and revert to the politics of liberalism. Shane Phelan's point is well taken: liberalism ignores our identities but the "nonnegotiable" identities of identity politics enslave us. The solution to this situation for these critics, however, is not to return to liberalism but, rather, to address the problems of identity politics. These attempts take different forms. Many critics of identity

3. Matsuda agrees with this analysis in her examination of the formation of the Asian-American coalition (1996, 179).

politics argue for some kind of coalition politics that retains many of the features of identity politics. Others offer defenses of identity politics by addressing the problems that its critics have identified and arguing for the positive elements of the practice.

Perhaps the most influential contemporary defense of identity politics is the position falling under the label *the politics of recognition*. Developed most extensively by the critical theorist Axel Honneth (1992, 1995), the politics of recognition expands on Hegel's belief that individuals' claim to intersubjective recognition of their identity is built into social life from the beginning. Honneth's goal is to develop Hegel's thesis that for every subject, the experience of being loved constitutes a necessary precondition for participation in the public life of the community. Love is necessary to successful ego development; it produces the basic self-confidence necessary to political participation. As Honneth puts it, "Without the feeling of being loved it would be impossible for the idea of an ethical community even to acquire what one might call inner-psychic representation" (1995, 38–39).

Although Honneth begins with Hegel's theory, he argues that it does not go far enough: Hegel anticipates the conception of ethical life based on the theory of recognition but does not take this step. In order to rectify this oversight, Honneth turns to George Herbert Mead. Mead's thesis is that human subjects owe their identity to the experience of intersubjective recognition. Combining Mead and Hegel, Honneth argues that the reproduction of social life is governed by the imperative of mutual recognition. Individuals can only develop a positive sense of self/identity when they have learned to view themselves from the perspective provided by society (92).

In the process of developing his thesis, Honneth refers to object relations theory as "well-suited to rendering love intelligible as the interactive relationship that forms the basis for a particular pattern of reciprocal relationships" (96). The position he takes is consistent with the theory of identity that I outlined in Chapter 1. He too sees object relations theory as providing important insights into the construction of identity. Like the object relations theorists, Honneth argues that one acquires one's identity through interaction with others in social relations: "In order to acquire a successful relation-to-self, one is dependent on the intersubjective recognition of one's attitudes and accomplishments" (136). Unlike the object relations theorists, however, Honneth explores the political implications of this position. If society reflects back to the individual a demeaning identity, then the individual cannot achieve a positive sense of self. It follows that society must provide each individual with such a positive sense of self, an identity grounded in respect and mutual recognition. If society fails to do so, then it must be "transformed."

Honneth uses this analysis to both explain and endorse the social movements that arose in the second half of the twentieth century. These movements were made up of social groups whose members were deprived of the love and recognition that Honneth is describing. The participants were demeaned by the identity they were assigned by the society in which they lived. Their political movement was an attempt to challenge that identity and to move toward the mutual recognition and respect to which they were entitled as members of society. Honneth concludes: "A conception of ethical life in terms of a theory of recognition precedes from the premise that the social integration of a political community can only succeed to the degree to which it is supported, on the part of members of society, by cultural customs that have to do with the way in which they deal with each other reciprocally" (58–59).

Several other critical theorists have advanced similar arguments. Jürgen Habermas, like Honneth, turns to Mead to argue that persons can only be individuals through socialization. He argues that it is thus a moral imperative of society to grant each individual respect, equality, and integrity. Habermas's discussion brings out a point that is only implicit in Honneth's account: the politics of recognition deconstructs the public/private distinction at the heart of liberalism. In arguing for a system of rights that is not blind to unequal social conditions, Habermas notes that "the color blindness of the selective reading vanishes once we recognize that we ascribe to bearers of individual rights an identity that is conceived intersubjectively. Persons, including legal persons, become individualized only through a process of socialization. A correctly understood theory of rights requires a politics of recognition that protects the integrity of the individual in the life contexts in which his or her identity is formed" (1998, 200). It is significant that Habermas illustrates his thesis by appealing to the history of feminism. From the outset, he maintains, feminists have been acutely aware of the "life context" in which identity is formed. The drive for equality in the feminist movement has always focused simultaneously on the public and private realms.

Nancy Fraser is also concerned about the politics of recognition, but her perspective departs from that of Honneth and Habermas. Fraser addresses what she calls the "decoupling" of cultural politics and social politics and the eclipse of the latter by the former (1997). The assumption of contemporary politics, she asserts, is that we must choose between class politics and identity politics. Fraser wants to correct this by developing a "critical theory of recognition," an approach that would integrate the social and cultural (5). While not denying the thesis of the politics of recognition, that recognition is necessary to human flourishing, she makes the point that economic injustice and cultural injustice are usually connected. Despite this connection, however, the strategies of redistribution and recognition have pulled in different directions. Redistribution policies dedifferentiate, while recognition policies increase differentiation.

Fraser's solution to this split is complex. She argues that there are two approaches to cultural injustice, an affirmative approach that positively affirms group identity and a transformative approach that works to transform the underlying cultural structure (24). Fraser wants to join the transformative approach to social politics: "Radical democrats will never succeed in untying the gordian knots of identity and difference until we leave the terrain of identity politics. This means resituating cultural politics in relation to social politics and linking demands for recognition with demands for redistribution" (174). Fraser concludes that justice demands the politics of recognition for some cases, the politics of redistribution for others (202).

Advocates of the politics of recognition argue that identity is formed socially and that the forces that shape identities are found throughout the social and political spectrum. This thesis is an important corrective to the theory of identity that informs liberalism. It is compatible with the theory of identity I have advanced here. But the politics of recognition does not answer some of the key questions raised by a politics of identity. The "politics" of the politics of recognition is too vague. It brings identity into the political sphere, but its advocates do not examine precisely what this identity might be. Specifically, advocates of the politics of recognition fail to provide a detailed understanding of the interface between what I am calling public and personal identities. The politics of recognition founders on the problem outlined by so many critics of the politics of identity: What is the identity that we bring into the political arena? How does this identity relate to the personal identity that we acquire, as both Mead and object relations theorists argue, from social interaction? We need to understand what public identities are and how they relate to personal identities before we can argue for a politics of recognition.

Another undertheorized aspect of the politics of recognition is the interface between the political and the social. If, as the advocates of this politics claim, identities are formed socially, then the political realm will not be the only or even the major target of resistance. This is not clear in the work of the authors cited in what precedes. They discuss the *politics* of recognition while their theory leads them to take a much broader perspective. The politics of recognition entails a strategy in which all aspects of society, not only the political, will be the target of resistance. It deconstructs the central tenets of liberalism, entailing a transformation of the liberal polity. Yet none of these entailments are clear from the writings of the advocates of the politics of recognition.

Another well-known argument for a politics of difference is that advanced by Iris Marion Young. In a series of books and articles Young has argued strongly for a politics that recognizes difference, that attempts to achieve justice through the acknowledgment of social groups and their relative disadvantage. In Chapter 2, I examined Young's position from the perspective of its relationship to liberalism. There I argued that the advantage of her perspective is that she makes it clear that the politics of difference entails jettisoning the central tenets of liberalism and conceiving of politics and justice in a radically different way. In sum, bringing identity into the public sphere entails taking difference seriously, rejecting universalism in favor of diversity.

Young's politics of difference would seem to embrace this tenet wholeheartedly. Young offers a convincing critique of the universalism of liberalism and the abstract citizen. There is much in her account that is an important corrective to liberalism. But Young does not go far enough in her critique. She rejects the universalism of liberalism but not universalism per se. Informing her argument for the politics of difference is the Habermasian assumption of the ideal of a communicative democracy in which groups agree on a universal conception of justice. In *Inclusion and Democracy* (2000) Young advances the thesis that political claims asserted from the specificity of a social-group position serve as a resource for, rather than obstruction of, democratic communication that aims at justice (82). She declares, "Differently situated actors create democratic publicity by acknowledging that they are together and they must work together to try to solve collective problems" (112). The key feature of the normative ideal of communicative democracy is the transformation of particular understandings of issues into "a more comprehensive understanding that takes the needs and interests of others more thoroughly into account" (113). This entails, she concludes, the move from a subjective to an objective way of looking at problems. Although she wants to distinguish her position from a "view from nowhere," Young nevertheless concludes, "Objectivity is an achievement of democratic communication that includes all differentiated social positions" (114).

Young's conception is clearly an improvement over liberalism. Her notion of the public realm is one that includes rather than rejects the partial and particular. But while rejecting the neutrality of liberalism, Young imposes another version of what she unabashedly labels "objectivity." Young presupposes that differently situated political actors can come together and agree on something called "justice." She assumes that participants in political discussions can and must make their claims understandable and persuasive to others; their discourse will be transformed from self-regard to appeals to justice (115).

In making this argument, Young is abandoning the "difference" aspect of the politics of difference. What her position comes to is that although the polity starts with difference, this difference is only a stepping stone to uniformity. She is reimposing a universal standard under which differences are subsumed. Her theory does not take into account the possibility, even probability, that all of us, groups or individuals, will not share a standard assumption about what constitutes a rational argument. This was the point make by Deveaux in her discussion of multiculturalism and, in a very different form, by Lyotard in *The Postmodern Condition: A Report on Knowledge* (1984). According to Lyotard, we live in a world in which there is no longer a single metanarrative to which we all subscribe. This includes Habermas's metanarrative of undistorted communication. Deveaux's argument is more specific but comes to the same thing. She asserts that certain social groups, particularly the disadvantaged groups that are the subject of Young's analysis, may not share the dominant groups' definition of what constitutes a rational argument in the political arena.

It is significant that Young herself advances a variant of this argument in another context. In a critique of deliberative democracy, Young argues that the theorists of this position assume a culturally biased conception of discussion that tends to silence some people or groups (1996, 122). Young's argument here is that what she calls "communicative democracy" avoids this problem because it recognizes the cultural specificity of deliberative practices. Communicative democracy, she argues, speaks *across* differences of culture. This argument appears to be in direct contradiction to her assertion in *Inclusion and Democracy* that "objectivity" is the achievement of democratic communication. It light of this later argument, it is hard not to conclude that for Young there is still an ideal of justice on which all can agree if only we could communicate in a context of equality and lack of coercion. She is not willing to accept the possibility that this ideal is no longer viable and that difference cannot, ultimately, be transcended.[4]

This ideal is not the only residue of universalism that lingers in Young's argument. I noted in Chapter 2 that although Young maintains that identity is inessential and shifting, she also makes the point that individuals can reject certain identities while adopting others. Her thesis is that individuals construct their own identities on the basis of social group positioning (2000, 82). This formulation raises more questions than it answers. At worst, it presupposes a preexisting agent who chooses from among the identities open to her/him in a given social setting. At best, it reveals a failure to adequately theorize the re-

4. Jodi Dean (1996) makes a similar argument in her notion of "reflective solidarity." Seyla Benhabib's "post-Enlightenment defense of universalism," "interactive universalism," is another instance of this position (1992). Like Dean and Young, Benhabib wants to retain an element of universality within difference.

lationship between personal and public identities. Who is the agent who is doing the choosing? How is the identity of this agent constituted? Young leaves these crucial questions unanswered.

Also unanswered is the question of why individuals choose to identify with one group rather than another. In *Inclusion and Democracy* Young makes the distinction between structural and cultural groups. Her point is that the difference between these two kinds of groups is frequently misunderstood, and she notes that the identity assertions of cultural groups usually appear in the context of structural relations of privilege and disadvantage (2000, 100). True enough. But implicit in Young's argument is the assumption that identification with structural groups is a given, a necessary aspect of social relations of power; other kinds of group identifications, it would seem, are not. But is this the case? Why am I required to identify with my structural group? Can I not place another identification, for example, race or gender, above that of class? Once more, Young's universalistic presuppositions creep into her theory of difference. Structural relations of power for Young are objective facts of social reality. They are not subject to the vagaries of perception and social construction. Rather, they constitute the bedrock of society.

On the face of it, it would seem that the theorists who adopt Judith Butler's position on identity would be prohibited from offering defenses of identity politics. But this has not been the case. Some theorists who adopt a Butleresque stance have argued that identity politics should not be completely abandoned. Kathy Ferguson, for example, argues for a coalition politics that does not replace identity politics but displaces it (1993, 186). The identities that would make up coalition politics, she claims, would be "mobile subjectivities," unstable categories, shaky representations. Coalition politics as Ferguson envisions it cannot turn completely from identity, but it will always keep identity in motion. For Ferguson, coalition politics is predicated on the belief that some people have enough in common to use the first-person plural pronoun (181).

Other theorists have advanced compatible theories. Eloise Buker argues for "hybrid selves" (1999). Shane Phelan states the case for coalitions based not on stable identities but on the recognition that "some social signifiers currently embody relations of oppression" (1997, 138). Following Butler, these theorists are arguing against any but the most minimal concept of identity. But these arguments have the effect of pointing to the need for identity rather than to its absence. As Ferguson puts it, there must be a "we" for any kind of politics to exist. Where does this "we" come from? Who are the individuals who become political agents who act in the political arena? By avoiding these questions, these theorists do not, as they hope, obviate the need to answer questions of identity. Rather, they emphasize the necessity of identity.

The closely linked issues of the multiplicity of identity and the necessity of coalition politics are at the center of many discussions of identity politics, particularly among feminists. It is abundantly obvious that women have multiple identities. The problem is how they can choose from among the different identity politics that represent those differences in their identities. The solution to this question, a solution that is popular in current discussions, is coalition politics.[5] But coalition politics does not solve the questions raised by identity politics; it simply moves them to a new location. Coalitions presuppose that there are identity groups that come together to form the coalition. But this begs the question of how we choose which group best represents our identity or whether choosing one group privileges it over the other aspects of our identity.[6]

My goal in this overview of the critiques and defenses of identity politics has been to emphasize the complexities of the issues raised by identity. Bringing identity into the political sphere changes everything. It necessitates a redefinition of citizenship, the political, and the nature of political action. Unless we understand the complexities of identity, particularly the relationship between personal and public identities, we cannot understand the role of identity in politics or the significance of identity politics in the contemporary polity. In the following section, I will develop this more complex understanding.

Personal and Public Identities: "It's a Girl!"

> Our identity is a specific marker of how we define ourselves
> at any particular moment in life. Discovering and claiming
> our unique identity is a process of growth, change, renewal
> and regeneration throughout our lifetime. As a specific marker,
> identity may seem tangible and fixed at any given point. Over
> the life span, however, identity is more fluid.
>
> —Gwen Kirk and Margo Okazawa-Rey,
> *Women's Lives: Multicultural Perspectives*

> I assume that identities are partly subjectively determined and
> partly objectively imposed and that the mix of these two varies
> from one context to another; that people sometimes experience
> their identities as given, sometimes as chosen, and sometimes

---

5. I will discuss this issue further in Chapter 4.
6. For a useful perspective on these issues, see Bickford 1996, 1997, 1999.

a combination of the two; that the meaning and salience of a given identity varies from one person to another among those who share the identity, and may shift over time in both respects both for the group as a whole and for individual members within it; that people often have multiple identities, each of which may have all of the preceding characteristics; and that group identities may or may not reflect cultural differences between groups (and can be quite powerful even when they do not).

—Joseph Carens, *Culture, Citizenship, and Community:*
A Contextual Exploration of Justice as Evenhandedness

The first of these two passages is from an introductory women's studies textbook. It is representative of the confusions about identity that characterize many approaches to the issue in contemporary feminist writing. The most important confusion evident here is whether identity is essential or constructed. According to Kirk and Okazawa-Rey, identity is, on the one hand, discovered and claimed and, on the other, fluid and changing. It is both a specific marker of who we are and an evolving process. Exactly how these contradictory elements fit together in the concept of identity is not specified either in the introduction or the body of the text.[7]

The second passage is from a book on multiculturalism and politics by Joseph Carens. Caren's passage is more sophisticated than that of Kirk and Okazawa-Rey. In it he covers the broad range of issues raised by identity: determination, imposition, construction, meaning, fluidity, individual and group influences, multiple identities. The passage indicates that Carens is sensitive to the complexity of issues that are raised by identity. What is significant, however, is that Carens never elaborates on the issues he raises here. This passage is a prelude to his discussion of culture and community in a political context. He is acknowledging the complexity of the issue of identity but implies that these issues need not be explored in order to examine issues of multiculturalism and identity politics.

These issues must be dealt with if we are to understand and assess identity politics. The contradictions and complexities of our concept of identity are central to what identity is all about. The central contradiction of identity is

7. Other examples of this confusion are not difficult to find. In a recent edited volume, *Identity Politics in the Women's Movement* (Ryan 2001), there is no attempt to precisely define the parameters of identity or to address any of the issues concerning the relationship between identity and politics that I have raised here.

that all of us experience our identity as both uniquely ours and as imposed by society. We need a theory that does not so much dissolve this contradiction as explore the intersection of uniqueness and determinism. To understand both identity and identity politics, we need to do more than list the complexities of identity. We need to examine them in detail.

Since we are faced with a philosophical question, it seems appropriate to turn to a philosophical analysis of that question. The male Anglo-American philosophical establishment has, indeed, had much to say about the question of identity.[8] But there is a curious myopia in these philosophical discussions of identity. Identities for these philosophers appear to exist in a vacuum. Individual identities are self-enclosed. They have no interaction with other identities or the society in which the identity is located.

Robert Nozick's discussion of identity is a good example of this. Nozick begins his analysis of identity by stating, "We want to understand not only the kind of being we are, but also what constitutes our individual identity as a particular kind of thing" (1981, 27). The aspect of identity that occupies Nozick's attention is bodily continuity. He is concerned with the question of whether bodily continuity is a necessary condition of personal identity. What if my mind were placed in someone else's body? Would I still be the same person? Nozick's answer to this question is his theory of the "closest continuer": "The closest continuer view holds that y at t2 is the same person as x at t1, only if, first, y's properties at t2 stem from, grow out of, are causally dependent on x's properties at t1, and, second, there is no other z at t2 that stands in a closer (or as close) relationship to x at t1 than y at t2 does" (36–37). Having established the theory of the closest continuer, Nozick asks is why the closest continuer, when it exists, gets special caring. In other words, why do I care about myself and, specifically, my future self when it is "simply (merely?) my current self's closest continuer?" (66) This question occupies Nozick for many pages. He seems to be genuinely puzzled by it.

The most charitable way to assess this analysis of identity is to claim that Nozick is concerned with an aspect of identity that does not arise from the social and political perspective I am adopting here. But I think this is too generous. Suggesting that philosophers such as Nozick are looking at identity from another perspective, the individual rather than the social, lets them off too easily. Identities, as I will argue below, cannot be understood in isolation. They are necessarily embedded and constituted in complex ways by the myriad forces of society. Viewing individual identity in isolation is not just another perspective, it is wrong. Nozick's individual is the autonomous, rational chooser that

8. The following analysis does not apply to most continental and feminist philosophers.

informs liberalism's abstract citizen. Defining individual identity as isolated from society results in a distorted view of identity. The fact that Nozick's individual has to *consider* whether to care for himself [*sic*] is a good indication of this distortion.

A dictionary provides a bit more help in unraveling the conundrums of identity. The *Oxford English Dictionary (OED)* informs us that *identity* and *identical* have the same root, the Latin *idem*, "the same." It then offers the following two definitions of *identity*:

> 1. The quality of being the same in substance, composition, nature, properties, or in particular qualities under consideration; absolute or essential sameness; oneness . . .

> 2. The sameness of a person or thing at all times and in all circumstances; the condition or fact that a person or thing is itself and not something else; individuality, personality.

Identity, in the English language, is a paradoxical concept. It connotes both sameness and uniqueness at the same time. The second definition of *identity* in the *OED* defines what most of us would call personal identity. It defines having an identity, being an individual, as being the same as oneself over time. Thus sameness defines uniqueness as an individual. The fact that I am the same as I was yesterday or ten years ago means that I am a unique individual. If I changed over time I would loose this uniqueness. People who lack this sameness are not defined as having an identity. This is the aspect of identity that concerns philosophers such as Nozick.

But the first definition of the term here reveals another aspect of identity: "the quality of being the same in substance, composition, nature, properties, or in particular qualities under consideration; absolute or essential sameness; oneness." This shifts the emphasis away from uniqueness and toward sameness, but a sameness with others, not oneself. When we are trying to determine the identity of some thing or things, we attempt to fit it under a general category. We attempt to *identify* its particular characteristics as the same as those of the other members of some category. We thus identify something as belonging to a general category because it shares characteristics with the members of that category. Here identity is derived not from uniqueness but sameness, from being a member of a general category.

The *OED* definition of *identity*, thus, leads to the conclusion that there are two distinct but related ideas embedded in our concept. The first definition refers to what I have been calling public identity. These are the general categories under which individuals are subsumed by the discourse of the society in which they live. Thus my "identity" in this society is that I am a woman, a professional, middle class, a suburbanite, white, heterosexual, and so on. These categories define my identity in my society. I have some control over my classification under these categories (more on this later) but much of it is simply a function of the way societies and languages operate. Languages creates general categories under which particulars are subsumed; many of these general categories involve people. Societies in turn institutionalize these general categories of people, assigning them specific meanings and hierarchies. These meanings have the effect of structuring societies in particular ways that vary from society to society.

The second definition of identity is what I have been calling personal identity. Each of us possesses what the object relations theorists call a core self. It is a self that is formed in relation to significant others in the early years of life. Despite its social constitution, however, this core self is stable. It persists over time; it remains the same day after day, year after year. In this limited sense, philosophers such as Nozick are right: to be an individual is to be the same over time. To lack this core self is to lack the ability to function in the world. This is the point made by theorists such as Lynn Layton and James Glass.

It is my thesis that these two definitions of identity are distinct yet related in complex ways. The goal of the following analysis is to explicate some of those complexities. It is also my thesis that confusing these two senses of identity has led to many of the misunderstandings about identity politics. *Identity* has been made to do too much work in our vocabularies. Identity politics is about the first sense of identity, the public categories under which we are subsumed. These public categories have a profound effect on the formation of our personal identities. This is the point of many feminists' analyses of "woman" and its effects on our identities. But public identities and personal identities are not identical. Failing to recognize the distinction between these two senses of identity leads to serious misunderstandings. Identity politics is about challenging, reaffirming, and redefining the public categories. It is about the first, not the second, definition of identity.

I should be clear at the outset, however, that I am not arguing for a dichotomy between personal and public identity. This is the bifurcated self of liberalism that I am challenging. What I am arguing is that personal and public identities are intricately related, and that what, through a process of social interaction, becomes personal identity is profoundly affected, although not monolithically determined, by public categories. I am also arguing, against the postmoderns, that we need to have a way to talk about personal identity that, as the dictionary describes it, persists over time. We need to be able to theorize that identity, the public categories that structure the social world, and the interaction between the two.

I will begin my explication of this thesis by building on the theory of identity presented in Chapter 1. There I argued that identity is constituted relationally in early childhood through interactions with primary caregivers. Out of this interaction a core self emerges, a sense of personal identity that provides individuals with a stable sense of self. One of the primary theses I argued in this context is that individuals are embedded in society and that this embeddedness constitutes their identity. But I also argued that embeddedness is always particular. I am embedded in society at a particular location, interacting with particular others. Although everyone is embedded, everyone's embeddedness is not the same.

Let me give an example of how I think this embeddedness works. I am born into a particular society that has assigned an identity to the category "woman." "Woman" is defined as inferior to "man," as irrational, nurturing, closer to nature, more emotional, and so forth. This is the public identity I am assigned. I will encounter this identity as I interact with others in society. I may not encounter all aspects of this identity in every social interaction. I may only encounter certain elements of it; at times I may seem free of it entirely. But it is always a factor in every woman's life in this society. Marilyn Frye (1983) has an apt metaphor to describe the workings of this public identity. She compares it to the bars on a birdcage. Each bar, each element of the public identity, is insignificant in and of itself. It is, admittedly, meaningless when a man opens a door for a woman. But cumulatively, the bars restrain the bird, keeping it in its cage. So do the elements of the public identity of "woman."

This public identity is constitutive because of my embeddedness in society. Its influence is pervasive; it structures what it means to be a woman in this society. In this I am in accord with social determinists such as Butler. But I want to complicate this theory by arguing that each of us will encounter this public identity from a particular location in this society. Although we will all be affected by it, it will be translated to each of us by the individuals and groups that structure our particular situation. The public identity, in other words, will be filtered through the lenses of our particular social locatedness. There are many elements to that filter. Although we can identify the principal filters, we cannot assert that in every case each of these filters will operate in the same way. In any given case, certain of these filters will predominate over others. There is no universal formula dictating how these filters work. But they will work to particularize the version of the public identity that each of us absorbs.

One of the major filters through which the pubic identity of "woman" passes is race. The translation of "woman" I encounter will be different if I am white,

Hispanic, African American, or Asian American. There is a rich literature by women of color exploring how race constitutes identity and how this constitution affects women of different ethnicities. This literature has transformed feminists' understanding of how the concept "woman" operates in society. The work of Gilligan cited in Chapter 1, furthermore, is an attempt to explore this filter. The girls Gilligan studied were all affected by the public identity of "woman." Indeed, they were grappling with how to become "women" as they passed through puberty. But Gilligan's work also demonstrates that the different racial/ethnic backgrounds of these girls profoundly affected the version of this public identity that they absorbed. For African American girls, independence was stressed. For Hispanic girls, ties to family and community were predominant. These filters produced different versions of the public identity "woman" that contributed to the formation of each girls' identity.

Another major filter is class. Gilligan's work also demonstrates the influence of this filter. The predominantly working-class girls whom she studied assimilated a concept of "woman" that was structured by their class position. In many cases, this concept/identity was in sharp contrast to the concept assimilated by the upper-middle-class girls whom Gilligan had studied in her earlier work. The working-class girls were effected by the vision of "woman" projected on their TV screens, the superwoman with the flying hair who balances career and family while looking glamorous. But these girls also realized that this ideal was not available to them in the same way it was to upper-middle-class girls. Their expectations were defined, at least in part, by the limitations imposed by their class position.

Another filter is family. Each of us is deeply affected by the particular structure of the family into which we are born and the character of the individuals who constitute this family. There are many elements to this filter. Some families are composed of biological parents and their offspring, although this model is no longer the norm. Some include extended family members. Some families are single parent, some what the sociologists call blended families. Some children are raised by a gay parent or parents. Some are raised in foster homes. Once more, there is no universal framework. What is universal, however, is the pervasiveness of the influence of family or its lack. It is in the family that the individual's core identity is formed. Its influence is always constitutive.

It follows that the differences and complexities of families are fundamental to the constitution of personal identity. Where an individual finds herself in the list I offered, or in a situation I did not think to list, will structure the version of "woman" that she will absorb. I will not pursue all these differences here. Instead, following the lead of object relations theory, I will concentrate on the mother-daughter relationship. For the vast majority of girls, their mother is not only the primary caretaker in early years but also the person through whom they learn to be a "woman." The mother translates for her daughter the public identity of "woman." The daughter's identity as a woman is shaped to a large degree by the version of "woman" that the mother communicates to her.

But mothers do not communicate a uniform message. Some mothers neatly conform to the public identity of "woman" that dominates our gender consciousness and communicate this identity to their daughters. These mothers will teach their daughters to conform to that identity, not to attempt to go beyond the boundaries it defines. This can have the effect of producing conforming daughters. Or it can have the opposite effect. The daughter may assimilate the conforming identity or rebel against it. Rebellion may be produced by, for example, the presence of a father who, implicitly or explicitly, encourages his daughter to exceed the boundaries that his wife is trying to impose on her. Studies of professional women of the post–World War II generation have shown a predominant influence of supporting fathers. Rebellion can also be generated by a nonconforming aunt or female teacher. Although the mother's influence in these cases cannot be discounted, the countervailing force of others provides the daughter with a means to transcend gender boundaries.

Another possible scenario is that of the nonconforming mother. This mother will attempt to teach her daughter not to incorporate the gender identity "woman" that is dominant in society. She will teach her daughter to rebel, to resist that identity, to create "gender trouble." The reasons that the mother is herself nonconforming probably have to do with *her* mother and her social experiences. In any case, the version of "woman" that this daughter assimilates will differ greatly from that communicated by the conforming mother. And, as with the conforming mother, either this identity training will take or it will backfire. The daughter may also become a gender rebel, following in her mother's footsteps. Or she may see the price her mother has had to pay for her rebellion and judge it too high. But in either case, the influence of the mother's version of "woman" will be constitutive.

These are only two possible scenarios. There are countless others. My point is that the mother's filter is crucial to the particular version of "woman" that the daughter integrates into her core identity. Furthermore, the influence of the mother will also be affected by the other filters of race and class. The public identity "woman" affects all of us. It is pervasive, hegemonic. But it is translated to each of us by the particular others who raise us. This translation will produce infinite variations on that identity. Because of the influences of, among others, race, class, and family characteristics, each of us will have a different take on the gender identity that defines "woman" in our society. We all manifest the identity "woman," but we do so in myriad ways.

There are four significant advantages to conceptualizing the formation of personal identity in this way. First, if we define personal identity as formed by the influence of public categories of identity filtered through the lenses of factors such as race/ethnicity, class, and family, we can explain both overarching patterns in identity and individual variation. We would expect to find, and, indeed, do find, that "women" in a given society will share certain broad characteristics. We will be able to identity commonalities among women that are a function of the dominance of the public category. Identifying and exploring these commonalities among women has been one of the major concerns of the contemporary feminist movement. The hegemony of "woman" has been carefully documented and examined by several generations of feminists.

The problem with these examinations is that they cannot account for the variations among women that also occur and, most notably, why some women conform and others rebel. The theory I am presenting here can accommodate these differences. It can explain why some women do not neatly conform to the hegemonic concept. They have, for reasons relating to their particular situation, rejected the public category, resisting its strictures. They are the variations from the general pattern, the gender rebels—the feminists—who resist the public category "woman" and create gender trouble.

Put another way, each of us forms a personal identity out of the discursive mix available to us in childhood. This mix will be different for each individual but will also exhibit societal patterns. It will even be different for siblings within a particular family. Identity is socially constituted, but the particular social location of each individual is different. This accounts for the uniqueness of individual identity and the differences between identities.

A second advantage of the perspective I am presenting here is that it can account for something that all of us know from daily life: the experience of possessing a stable personal identity. When each individual's core self is formed, it is experienced as a unique personal possession. I *am* my identity. Although, in an analytic mode, I can examine the social, racial, class, and familial influences that constitute my identity, in everyday life I experience that identity not as determined by hegemonic social forces and personal influences but as *mine*. This is an important element of identity that is often overlooked in theoretical discussions, particularly those of the postmoderns. Unless I experience my identity as my possession, unless I see myself not as a social dupe but as an agent acting in my world, I cannot function in that world. To be a competent adult in any society I must experience myself as possessing a core identity.

Social determinists such as Butler find this experiential aspect of identity difficult to acknowledge for several reasons. They are uncomfortable talking about unique personal identity because it appears to be a retreat to the modernist subject. Just as important, they cannot integrate the concept of personal identity with the cultural determinist position they espouse. Social dupes do not have unique identities; by definition they perform the script of the public identity. Against this I am arguing that we need a theory that can accommodate both personal and public identity.

The third, and perhaps most significant, advantage of this theory is that it provides a way to understand the phenomenon of identity politics. Although personal and public identities can never be neatly separated, identity politics primarily addresses public, not personal identity. The "identity" of identity politics concerns the public categories under which we, as members of a particular society, are subsumed. Although an individual's personal, identity is profoundly shaped by these public categories, it is not identical to it. We all posses both personal and public identities.

The relationship between personal identity and the public categories that define identity politics can take many different forms. Once more the women's movement in the contemporary United States provides a useful illustration. The concept "woman" that informs the women's movement is not the "woman" of the public, hegemonic category. It is, instead, a rebellion against that definition, an attempt to redefine what it is to be a woman in our society. Quite clearly, all women have not embraced the women's movement. On the contrary, most women in the United States do not define themselves as feminists. They reject the redefinition of "woman" that this movement represents.

Why, then, do some women join the women's movement, defining themselves as feminists, and others do not? To be a feminist is to *identify* elements of one's core self with the redefinition of "woman" that the women's movement represents. Women who define themselves as feminists are women who rebel against the strictures of the public category "woman." They are gender rebels who do not conform to that definition. Furthermore, they find the redefinition of "woman" that the women's movement represents compatible with elements of their personal identity. In other words, they *identify* with this redefinition because it accords with elements of their core selves, elements forged by their personal experiences.

This process of identification also characterizes racial or panethnic identity politics. The purpose of identity politics in this context is to positively affirm the public category. To engage in, for example, African American identity politics is to publicly affirm this aspect of one's identity. Like the women's movement, this affirmation involves redefining the "public identity" category. Racial and panethnic identity politics are engaged in the task of redefining negative stereotypes. Participants in these forms of identity politics attempt to bring a positive racial/ethnic identity to the political forefront. This is no mean feat. Typically, it involves combating negative perceptions deeply rooted in the culture. But it is quite clearly a process involving public, not personal, identity.

My thesis, then, is that the relationship between personal and public identity manifest in identity politics is a process of identification between personal and public identities. Identity politics is about public identity. If I perceive that elements of a public identity resonate with my personal identity, I am motivated to *identify* with the political movement of a particular identity group. Because this identity is a public category, it will not precisely match my personal, unique identity. There are necessarily elements of my personal identity that are not represented by the identity group. I do not and cannot bring my whole personal self to the movement. But in joining the political movement of an identity group, I bring a part of myself into the public arena and identify with that public identity.

Although I am asserting that identity politics is primarily concerned with public identity, I also want to stress that we should never lose sight of the interface between public and personal identity. Changing the public identity under which I am subsumed will have a profound effect on my personal identity. This is why people engage in identity politics in the first place. As the advocates of the politics of recognition rightly emphasize, one needs to live in a world that reflects back to one a positive public identity. The point of engaging in identity politics is to achieve that end. Thus even though the focus of identity politics is the public category, its goal is to define a more positive personal identity for the participants in that politics.

In a sense, it seems too easy to resolve some of the central questions of identity politics simply by defining it as a process of identification. For anyone actually involved in identity politics, joining a political group defined in terms of identity *seems* like an affirmation of one's personal identity. It seems like "going public" with this personal identity. But if we look, in a Wittgensteinian sense, at what we are actually doing in this situation, another interpretation emerges. Joining a political movement is a public act. It concerns the sameness aspect of the definition of identity, not the unique aspect. By joining a political group defined by identity, I am identifying with a public definition that subsumes me. This identification is related to my personal identity in the sense that it resonates with some aspect of that identity. But it is not and cannot be the same as my personal identity. The two aspects of identity operate on different planes.

The fourth advantage of conceptualizing identity and identity politics in this way is that it focuses on power. Identity politics is about power, its institution, our resistance to it, our redefinition of it. I am not claiming that other approaches to identity ignore the role of power. Clearly Judith Butler, Wendy Brown, and many other critics of identity politics define the imposition of a particular identity as an act of power. The advantage of the approach I am advocating is that it brings the role of power to the forefront by juxtaposing personal and public identity.

"There is difference and there is power. And who holds the power decides the meaning of the difference" (Jordan 1994, 197). June Jordan's comment here has important implications for the analysis of identity politics. Identity politics is about difference. It began as a protest against the allegedly "neutral citizen" that erased all differences within the category. The power of this erasure is profound. Under the guise of universality, the "neutral citizen" created a political hierarchy in which some were more "citizen" than others. Identity politics constitutes a resistance to this power, an argument that the public category "citizen" is misconceived precisely because it erases differences.

The advent of identity politics has not erased the connection between difference and power. I argued in Chapter 2 that the hegemonic power of liberalism has distorted identity politics by subsuming all its participants under the rubric of "others." This effectively marginalizes all participants in identity politics, separating them from the "real" citizens who do not have identities. Another manifestation of hegemonic power is the fixing of identity that is presumed to occur in identity politics. This fixing is a function of liberalism; it is not inherent in identity politics. Liberal politics forces the participants in identity politics to assume a common identity. They must enter the public arena as "women." "African Americans," "lesbians," and so on. Not only do they have identities whereas normal citizens do not, no differences are allowed within the identity group.

In her essay on what freedom means in a feminist context, Nancy Hirschmann argues that while feminists must continue to emphasize social construction, we must also keep in mind that some groups of people "systematically and structurally" have more power to do the constructing than others (1996, 60). Identity politics is a challenge to those groups that systematically and structurally have the power to define us, subsume us under public identity categories, and specify what those categories mean. But although identity politics constitutes an important challenge to this hegemonic power, it has not curbed it. Toleration is a form of power as well. By tolerating identity politics, the liberal polity has also succeeded in controlling it. The liberal polity has neatly subsumed identity politics without changing the fundamental structure of that polity. We need to be aware of this aspect of power as well.

Elements of the thesis I am presenting here have been advanced in the debates over identity and identity politics. In her influential book, *"Am I That Name?"* (1988), Denise Riley argues that "woman" is an unstable category and that this instability is a historical fact that feminism must accept. Her suggestion is that even though there is no essential identity to "woman," feminist politics should operate as if "woman" existed, because the world in which we live operates on that assumption. "Woman," she asserts, is historically and discursively constructed, a "volatile collectivity" (2). What Riley is attempting to do is bridge the gap between an identity politics that is necessarily grounded in "woman" and the deconstructive insight that there is no essential identity to "woman." Her solution: "I'd argue that it is compatible to suggest that 'women' don't exist—while maintaining a politics of 'as if they existed'—since the world behaves unambiguously as if they did" (112). She hopes that over time what she calls this "rigid opposition" between philosophical correctness and strategic necessity will loosen.

In another context, Riley returns to this thesis by arguing that an aspect of any feminism must be the "collective self-consciousness of 'being women.'" She refers to this as an "elective identification" (122). Riley's position is consistent with much of what I have argued above. It is the world's (society's) concept of "woman" that we are resisting in feminist politics. This concept is very real. It shapes our identity; it constitutes the boundaries of our agency. To join the feminist movement is to identify with another definition of "woman," a concept that contests society's definition. None of these definitions are essential. All are historical and social constructs. But they are also very real in the sense that they constitute who we are; they create reality for us.

What is missing in an account such as Riley's, however, is a consideration of personal identity. Who is this being who identifies with the feminist movement, who resists the societal definition of "woman"? The reluctance to talk about the individual who is constituted by the public category "woman" is pervasive in contemporary feminist theory. Butler's influence here has been definitive. Discussions of personal identity and individual agency are suspect because they conjure up the specter of the modernist subject. Even when the topic under discussion is political agency in identity politics, this restriction applies. In her extensive analysis of the relationship between identity and politics, for example, Jodi Dean is concerned with the way in which "society" affects "individuals," the "specific problematization of identities" (1996, 217, 221). But although she argues that exploring this relationship is a necessary task, Dean does not provide this analysis. There is no examination of how personal identity is formed, why certain kinds of individuals exist and others do not, or how socialization varies across society.

There is a notable exception to this generalization. In *Not Only for Myself: Identity, Politics, and the Law* (1997), Martha Minow argues that people need an identity because it gives them a necessary sense of place and connection in the world. The problem Minow sets out to solve is how to strike a productive stance toward the paradoxes of individual and social meaning. The definition of identity that Minow proposes is that of a process of negotiation through social relationships of power and culture. The focus of her analysis is how social relations create identities and the oppression they stand for. Her approach is grounded in the claim that "none of us have individual identities except by reference to collective social experiences, and yet all of us retain some degrees of freedom for self-invention out of the found materials of biographical and social life" (23). Individuals, Minow argues, are members of multiple, intersecting groups. Each person is alone at the unique crossroads of intersecting groups. She concludes that this situation implies a profound challenge for identity politics (39). Identity politics fixes one aspect of these complex, unique identities. Particularly when courts and legislatures assign identity, the complexity and multiplicity of identity is denied and people's latitude to choose is cut off.

Minow proposes several solutions to remedy this situation. As an alternative to laws that protect persons with particular identities, she proposes focusing on harm done to individuals who are perceived in a specific way (80). She advocates diverse government policies that permit individuals to identify with groups temporarily and for specific purposes rather than a policy of fixed groups (94). Overall, her strategy is to combat group-based discrimination but also to "promote complications of group membership and identification" (151). What Minow is arguing for is best summarized in her distinction between the politics of "I am" and the politics of "I want" (55). Her thesis is that we should move from a politics of "I am," the presumption of contemporary identity politics, to a politics of "I want," a politics in which groups of citizens come together to achieve a particular goal.

Minow's perspective indicates how difficult it will be to conceptualize a polity in which identification rather than identity is at the root of political activity. The advent of identity politics has challenged the basic structure of the liberal polity. The notion that identity matters in politics, that the neutral citizen is not neutral, is an important first step in altering that polity. Minow is describing the next step. Her analysis reveals that we now need to engage in some difficult work in order to understand the role of identity in a redefined political arena. The foregoing analysis has been an attempt to accomplish this goal. My thesis is that we must understand that the identity we assume in the public realm is a public identification, not our personal (in Minow's terms, unique) identity. To engage in identity politics is to identify with a public identity, not to become that identity. This is an identification that can and will shift over time (Riley's point). We need a political system that acknowledges and legitimizes this identification but can also accommodate its shifting nature.[9]

Conclusion

> The public and the private worlds are inseparably con-
> nected; . . . the tyrannies and servilities of the one are the
> tyrannies and servilities of the other.
>
> —Virginia Woolf, *Three Guineas*

It should be clear from the foregoing discussion that my exploration of the relationship between personal and public identity is intended as a reinterpretation, not an endorsement of identity politics, particularly as it exists in the present-day United States. There is much that is wrong with this practice. Liberalism has thwarted the potential of identity politics to radically alter the liberal polity and, specifically, to move toward a conception of the embodied citizen. Identity politics as it exists in the United States has failed to transform the liberal polity. But it should also be clear that this potential has likewise been thwarted by the attitudes that the participants bring to identity politics. Many who participate in identity politics assume that it necessarily entails the fixing of personal identity to conform to the definition espoused by the identity group. In other words, they have bought into this politics an assumption that, I have argued, is a product of the structure of the liberal polity. The result is Phelan's "Lesbian" or its equivalent. Assuming that participation in identity politics entails the internal conformity of the identity group defeats the logic of this politics. The goal of identity politics is to challenge the public identities under which we are subsumed. Fixing the personal identities of the members of the identity group does not facilitate this goal.

I am aware, however, that moving from, in Minow's terms, a politics of "I am" to a politics of "I want" is not easy. It is difficult not to essentialize and ontologize the identity of groups, as the contemporary experience of identity politics amply illustrates. In many social situations it seems abundantly obvious that I am whatever identity I have been assigned by that situation. We need to resist this impulse. What I am is a complicated mix of the influence of my par-

---

9. Shachar's (2001) advocacy of "joint governance" is another attempt to recognize that we all identify with multiple groups and to devise legal strategies that reflect this fact.

ticular location and the public categories under which I am subsumed. Those public categories can never entirely encompass my particular identity. Identity politics should reflect this, not distort it by essentializing group identity.

Defining identity politics in terms of identification rather than identity accomplishes this goal. Identity politics is a challenge to or redefinition of public identity categories. To embrace identity politics is to *identify* with that public category. This identification typically takes the form of the resistance to a hegemonic category. In the case of feminist politics it entails a resistance to the hegemonic definition of "woman" and an identification with the feminist redefinition of that public category. It can also entail, in the case of racial/ethnic identity politics, a positive reaffirmation of the public identity. But in no case does it, nor should it, entail fixing personal identities. Joining an identity group is a declaration that I am challenging a public-identity category and that I want the changes that are entailed by that redefinition. It signifies that I want specific policies, not that I am a specific identity. All those who want these policies are not the same and may not even want them for the same reasons.

This perspective throws new light on the critic of identity politics discussed earlier who complained that it forced her to choose one aspect of her identity over another. She complained that she wanted to bring her whole self to the table but that the divisions of identity politics prohibited her from doing so. This is an example of the misunderstanding of identity politics that I am contesting. We all have complex identities. Participating in identity politics entails identifying one aspect of our personal identity with the goals of the movement. I cannot and should not bring my "whole self" to this endeavor. Political action and personal identity are related but also distinct. Joining the feminist movement is identifying with one aspect of my personal identity. Joining a racial/ethnic political movement is identifying with another aspect. Neither fixes my personal identity, because it is a public, political action.

Put another way, on one issue I may identify one aspect of my personal identity with one identity group, and on another issue with another identity group. I will shift between these groups depending on the issue at hand. This is what Minow means when she advocates a politics of temporary rather than fixed groups. But what I mean by *shifting* in this context is very different from the position espoused by Butler. Butler wants to do away with personal identity altogether. The shifting she advocates is based on the lack of identity, the definition of identity as fictive, performative. The shifting I am promoting is grounded in the existence of a stable personal identity. From my personal identity, I identify with one group on one cause and with another group on another. It is the base from which I engage in specific political action.

A central aspect of the relationship between personal and public identity is that it emphasizes the role of hegemonic power in identity politics. Identity politics is about contesting the public-identity categories that define us. This public identity is a social construction. It can be changed through political and other kinds of action. The fact that we are capable of contesting this public category means that we are not wholly defined by it. If we were, there would be no resistance. The 1960s feminists were right: the personal is political. Public categories define the parameters of personal identity. But it does not follow that public and personal identity are indistinguishable. According to Foucault, where there is power there is resistance. This is also both true and not. *Sometimes* there is resistance, and that sometime depends on the personal identities doing the resisting. Some individuals resist and others do not. The variable lies in the social construction of our personal identities.

My goal in this chapter has been to explore the interface of personal and public identity in order to understand the phenomenon of identity politics. By engaging in this analysis, however, I am also pursuing a broader aim: bringing together two theories of identity that, although true within the sphere they define, are both incomplete. The first is that of the original object relations theorists. These theorists are right that identity is formed in the social interactions of early childhood. Identity is socially constructed, not given. It is a product of the specific location of each individual child and the specific others who raise her. What is missing from this theory, however, at least in its original form, is an analysis of the larger social context in which the child exists. Core selves are formed through interaction with others, but those others do not exist in isolation. They communicate to us societally defined conceptions of who we are, what we can be, and how we should act.

The second theory of identity, in contrast, is exclusively concerned with the social context in which identities are formed. Social determinists such as Judith Butler argue that we are constituted by public categories such as "woman." Contemporary feminist theorists have extensively documented the nature and extent of this constitution. The theories of these thinkers have added immeasurably to our understand of how these categories operate in society. What these theories omit, however, is personal identity. We are constituted but not wholly determined by the social categories that they analyze. What I am arguing here is that we need to combine these two theories, to develop a theory of the interface of personal and public identity without losing the advantages of either. Gilligan's approach, particularly in her later work, goes a long way toward developing such a theory. My purpose here is to build on that approach and bring it into a specifically political context.

4

A New Politics of Identity

At the beginning of this study I argued that the problems associated with the issue of identity are both pervasive and complex. Our understanding of identity affects every aspect of our lives, from our personal sense of self to the public categories under which we are subsumed to the politics in which we engage. Changing those understandings, consequently, changes everything—individuals, politics, society. The complexity of the issues raised by identity, furthermore, entails that it is not possible to neatly separate these issues; they are related and interact in myriad ways. Most notably, we cannot separate personal and public identities, because they are intricately interrelated.

My task now is to bring the elements of my argument together. The connection between the theory of identity that I presented in Chapter 1—object relations theory—and the critique of the liberal individual I developed in Chapter 2 should be obvious. What is wrong with the liberal individual/citizen is that it is based on a denial of the social nature of identity. We are not and cannot be the autonomous, rational choosers that the liberal tradition presupposes. Nor can we be neutral and disembodied. Rather, as the object relations theorists argue, identities are social, particular, embedded, and connected. Liberalism refuses to acknowledge these foundations of identity.

If we "correct" liberalism in this respect, that is, if we replace the neutral, autonomous citizen with an embodied, particular and social citizen, then we must confront the problem I addressed in Chapter 3: the relationship between personal and public identity. Liberalism both veils and forbids identity. Particular identities do not belong in the public sphere. If we tear away the veil, recognize and legitimize identity, the nature of the political is radically altered. If identity politics is to succeed, it necessitates a careful definition of the new relationship between identity and politics. Many advocates of identity politics have failed to produce this definition. Many of the problems associated with that politics, consequently, can be traced to the failure to be clear about the nature of "identity" in the public sphere. Developing the theory of the interaction between hegemonic concepts and particular societal filters was my attempt to address this problem.

The logical next step must be to more specifically outline the parameters of the new politics of identity for which I am arguing. In Chapter 2, I asserted that bringing identity into the liberal polity transforms that polity. It challenges the abstract uniformity that defines liberalism and moves in the direction of radical pluralism. I also argued that multiculturalism as it has come to be defined in theory and practice is not the only option for a politics of identity. The politics of identity I envision will be based on identification, not fixed identity categories. I now want to argue that there is another sense in which identity politics transforms liberalism: it necessitates a new theory of power. Focusing on identity reveals that the forces that constitute our identities are everywhere; they transcend the strictly legal/political sphere. Identity politics thus forces us to look for the power that creates subjects/identity everywhere in society and to develop a theory of that power. It also forces us to develop a new strategy of resistance. If power is everywhere, so must resistance be. Resisting state power is not enough; resistance, like power, must be everywhere.

To explore these transformations and advance an alternative conception of power, I turn to the work of Michel Foucault. Using Foucault's definition of power in the contemporary world I argue for an understanding of identity politics that encompasses both the political and the social. This use of Foucault's work contradicts the accepted understanding of the relationship between his work and identity politics. Foucault's work is usually cited by the critics of identity politics to challenge the fixing of identity that it allegedly entails. Foucault's theory of the subject, like that of Butler's, is a subject lacking identity and agency, a social dupe. As I made clear in Chapter 1, this theory of the subject is incomplete because it does not allow for a conception of personal identity. Despite this, however, there is an aspect of Foucault's work that is useful to an analysis of identity politics: his theory of power and resistance. He offers a critique of the juridical concept of power that informs liberalism and develops an alternative conception. It is my intention here to analyze the phenomenon of identity politics from the perspective of this theory of power. Foucault's theory of power, a theory that extends power beyond the strictly political realm, is an important corrective to liberal theory and provides a unique perspective on the practice of identity politics. Although Foucault ultimately fails to fulfill the radical potential of his theory, he nevertheless lays the groundwork for a new conception of politics in general and identity politics in particular.

Many feminist critics of Foucault have argued that his work ignores issues of gender. This is undoubtedly true. Many feminists have also maintained that his work can nevertheless be usefully employed in exploring questions of how gender subordination is constructed and perpetuated. My argument is that Foucault's work is useful to feminist theory in another sense. His perspective on power and subordination provides an understanding of the relationship between women and state power that has significant implications for both feminist theory and identity politics. His work invites us to take the long view, to look at the constitution of power across centuries and millennia. His "history of the present" places the phenomenon of power in a historical perspective that extends to antiquity. If we examine the power relationship between women and the state from this long view, a notable pattern emerges: the history of the state, particularly in the West, and the history of the subordination of women are inextricably linked. It also emerges that this relationship is not the result of happenstance, but, rather, is deeply rooted in the nature and evolution of state power as it has developed in the West.

In her controversial book, *The Creation of Patriarchy* (1986), Gerda Lerner argues that the subordination of women was institutionalized in the first written legal codes in the Middle East. Previous to the emergence of these codes, in roughly 1750 B.C., the source of women's subordination was the patriarchal family. Lerner argues that the enactment of these laws, like that of all laws, is an indication that the practice it addresses existed and had become problematic (102). In this case, in other words, the control of women by the patriarchal family had become insufficient, and it was necessary for the state to step in and reinforce that control. One of the significant results of this development was that, from its inception, the archaic state recognized its dependence on the patriarchal family. And most important, the orderly functioning of the patriarchal family was equated with order in the public domain (121). Thus the patriarchal family was defined as the basic building block of political order. Specifically, the control of women's sexuality was the responsibility of the state;

punishment for deviation from the established code of sexuality was the state's obligation. The legal classification and regulation of women's sexual activities, Lerner argues, was a historical watershed.[1]

An examination of women's relationship to state power in the present-day United States suggests that we are at another historical watershed. One of the principal goals of the U.S. women's movement since the 1960s has been to remove the regulation and control of women's sexuality from the purview of the state. This effort has had significant success. Most, if not all, of the legal restrictions on women have been removed. In her analysis of the history of marriage in the United States, Nancy Cott (2000) documents this success. I cited Cott's analysis in Chapter 2 to support the argument that liberal citizenship is defined in masculine terms. But her analysis can also be used to document the gradual severing of the link between the subordination of women and state power. After enumerating the myriad ways in which marriage has constrained women throughout U.S. history, Cott then analyzes the series of legal decisions that have removed the majority of those restraints. According to Cott, the law establishes and maintains an "official morality" that, until recently, has been centrally defined in terms of marriage. In recent decades, however, the United States Supreme Court in particular has moved toward displacing marriage from the seat of that official morality (Cott 2000, 199). Cott writes, "This alteration between marriage and the state might be called 'disestablishment'" (212). Although she qualifies this conclusion by arguing that this disestablishment does not apply to homosexuals and that marriage continues to confer a privileged status, she nevertheless argues that the political role of marriage has evaporated as "ballast for the form of governance" (213). The contemporary view of marriage in the United States, Cott concludes, is that of a "private realm of family life which the state cannot enter" (1).

The current status of women in the United States according to Cott's assessment is in sharp contrast to the relationship between women and state power that has characterized the state since its inception. Most simply, the control of women and, specifically, the control of women's sexuality, has moved from its position as the pillar of state control, Cott's "ballast," to a marginal aspect of that power. We must be careful, however, not to overstate this severing of power. The second-class-citizen status of women is still implicit in many legal definitions. In an era of conservative politics, the reinstitution of legal restrictions on women is a continual threat. But it is nevertheless the case that the near

1. By using Lerner's work in this context I am not endorsing her argument as a whole, an argument that has been legitimately criticized by many historians. I am utilizing only one aspect of her thesis, the connection between the advent of the state and the control of women's sexuality. This point is well documented in her text.

complete removal of state power from the control of women is a change of historic proportions. Women continue to be constrained in contemporary U.S. society, but that constraint is now located primarily in the social rather than the strictly political/legal sphere. This change calls for a new political strategy, a dual strategy that targets the political and the social simultaneously.

This is where Foucault's work can be useful in an analysis of identity politics. First, Foucault outlines a conception of power that transcends the limited, juridical conception that informs liberal political theory. His formulation points beyond the political/legal sphere to the myriad aspects of social life as the sources of constraint and constitution. In the contemporary world, it is in this realm that identities are constituted; the identities that the adherents of identity politics seek to challenge have primarily social roots. Second, Foucault's theory of subjectification provides a means of understanding the constitution of those identities. In the terminology I have developed in my thesis, what Foucault is doing is describing the constitution of public identities. Although this conception is incomplete, it is valuable in that it carefully details the constitution of these identities and an understanding of how to resist the forces that create and distort them.

Power and the State

What I am arguing, then, is that in order to understand and resist the powers that constitute the identity "woman," and, by extension, all identities, we must move beyond the political/legal sphere and examine the broader social context in which public identities are formed. Foucault never specifically examines the subordination of women or the source(s) of their subjectification. But if we look at his theory from the perspective of this thesis, his work provides an analysis of the emergence and functioning of the new form of power that accomplishes this subordination. Foucault states very clearly that the goal of his work is to trace the evolution of a new form of power in Western society since the sixteenth century. This new form of power, he maintains, demands a form of analysis that is lacking in what he calls the juridical conception of power that dominates political theory. In the course of his discussion Foucault identifies several new forms of this power rather than one. This in itself is significant. He is not arguing, as did Marx, that power has shifted from one single location to another. Rather, power has become diffused. Instead of emanating from a single source, it is spread throughout every corner of society, informing the social structure as a whole.

Foucault's effort to trace the genealogy of these new forms of power leads him, first of all, to the Christian Church in the Middle Ages. He argues that the practices of the church developed a new kind of power that had the individual as its object: "This form of power applies itself to immediate everyday life which categorizes the individual, marks him by his own individuality, attaches him to his own identity, imposes a law of truth on him which he must recognize and which others have to recognize in him" (1983b, 212). Foucault asserts that this form of power, which he calls "pastoral power," was integrated into the modern Western state, turning that state into "[a] modern matrix of individualization, or a new form of pastoral power" (215).

Foucault has much to say about pastoral power, but for my purposes his most significant claim is that nonstate institutions, most notably the family, were mobilized to carry out pastoral power (215). In other words, as the Western state takes on a radically new function, overseeing the individuality of its subjects, the locus of power is diffused beyond the state to the institutions of civil society. And central among these institutions is the family, the source of most gender socialization and definition, the locus of the constitution of "woman."

One of Foucault's means of characterizing the workings of pastoral power is by the term "disciplinary power." The purpose of *Discipline and Punish* (1979) was to present a genealogy of this power, its effects and justifications. But Foucault's study is much more than a history of prisons. Prisons are, after all, state institutions. For Foucault, the prison, as a manifestation of state power, changed the nature of power itself. He argues that disciplinary relations "go right down into the depths of society, they are not localized in relations between the state and its citizens" (1979, 27). In the seventeenth and eighteenth centuries, disciplinary methods, which had been in existence in various social institutions, became general formulas of domination: "Discipline may be identified neither within an institution nor within an apparatus; it is a type of power, a modality for its exercise, comprising a whole set of instruments, techniques, procedures, levels of application, targets; it is a 'physics' or an 'anatomy' of power, a technology" (215).

Central to disciplinary power is the distinction between the normal and the abnormal. Disciplining subjects means channeling their behavior in the "right" direction and defining other activities as abnormal, deviant. This power of normalization is, for Foucault, diffused throughout society. But, significantly, it is, once more, the family that is crucial. The family, he argues, is the "privileged locus" of the emergence of disciplinary power. It is in the family that the essence of disciplinary power, the distinction between the normal and the abnormal, is defined and enforced (216).

Two themes dominate Foucault's discussion of disciplinary power. First, such power is radically incompatible with relations of sovereignty (1980c, 104). Disciplinary power is not a relationship between sovereign and subject but a network of power relations that permeates society. Second, as a consequence, the rise of disciplinary power forces us to look beyond the state if we want to understand power relations. The emblem of disciplinary power, the Panopticon, was not confined to prisons. It was in barracks, factories, schools, hospitals. The normalization that is the goal of disciplinary society is everywhere; the "judges of normality" pervade every aspect of society.

Although Foucault does not make this point, it is clear that the concept of normality is central to the disciplining of identities. Foucault is analyzing the process by which identities are created and maintained. Every identity in society is defined and then assigned the particular script that is deemed appropriate. The disciplinary mechanisms that Foucault describes are the means by which these definitions are enforced and become hegemonic. The family is key here, but the role of other, nonstate institutions is constitutive as well.

Pastoral power entails oversight of the whole individual, encompassing every aspect of his/her life. The disciplinary mechanisms that begin to permeate Western society are one aspect of pastoral power. Another is what Foucault calls "bio-power." In the eighteenth century, Foucault claims, the interest in the population extends to "power over life" (1980c, 226). Biopower designates "what brought life and its mechanisms into the realm of explicit calculations and made knowledge-power an agent of transformation of human life" (1980b, 143). Instead of dealing with individuals in terms of their juridical/legal status, governments, through the police, dealt with them as living beings—working, trading, living (1988b, 156). "One might say that the ancient right to *take* life or *let* live was replaced by a power to *foster* life or *disallow* it to the point of death" (1980b, 138).

In his study *The Policing of Families* (1979), Jacques Donzelot supplies further evidence of this development. He argues that the aim behind state control of the family was to reconcile the interests of families and the state and that this was accomplished through the moralization of behavior within the family. He documents a transition from "a government of families to a government through the family" (92). Two aspects of this change are significant. First, one of the keys to the transition was not the government per se but the doctor working in conjunction with the government. It was the doctor who, in Foucault's terms, pronounced on normalcy. Second, the tool of the doctor's power in the family was the mother. Ironically, the mother, as the executor of the doctor's prescriptions, gained influence and, consequently, so did women as a whole.

One of the most innovative aspects of Foucault's thesis is the connection between biopower and the modern human sciences. Central to the deployment of biopower was knowledge of the population that was to be controlled. The government had to know everything about its subjects in order to govern their lives in the sense demanded by biopower. Aggregate characteristics of the population had to be available to facilitate the formulation of policies to govern that population. A new discourse—statistics—evolved to meet this need, and this discourse became central to the evolving human sciences. The technology of statistics made it possible for governments to create a reality—the statistical facts of their populations—that they could then control. The population was defined as a reality possessing certain statistically defined characteristics that could be addressed by government policies (Hunter 1996, 154). Statistics became one of the major mechanisms by which the government defined and maintained the "normal." Thus the rise of the human sciences, the discourses whose object is the individual, was inextricably linked to the rise of biopower.

It is significant for my thesis that Foucault identifies the most effective and characteristic manifestation of biopower as the control of sexuality. He argues that in the nineteenth century a discourse of sexuality developed; the subject became a scientific question that produced knowledge and truth. He spends a good deal of time analyzing how the discourse of sexuality is deployed. The keys to this power are educational and psychiatric institutions and, again, the family (1980b, 46). His central point is that the expansion of power over sex was deployed in a way "quite different" from the way in which the law operated. Such power is distinct from the juridical power of sovereign and subject: "never have there existed more centers of power; never more attention manifested and verbalized; never more circular contacts and linkages; never more sites where the intensities of pleasures and the persistency of power catch hold, only to spread elsewhere" (49). Although this power originated with the state, because its character was so different from the juridical power of the state, it took on a life of its own. It spread throughout society, transforming the singular power of the state into a different form altogether.

Foucault claims that he is not offering a "theory" of power but only a description of a field of analysis (1988a, 38). This claim makes little sense. Foucault offers much more than a description of this new form of power. He develops a sophisticated theoretical understanding of it and, most important, defines a means of resisting its influence. The first step in his project is an understanding of contemporary political theory and the juridical conception of power it espouses. The juridical conception of power is negative—it defines power only in terms of prohibitions. Juridical power is, of course, the foundation of liberalism, famous for its definition of freedom as "freedom from." Because juridical power defines power as limited to the state, it misses the myriad deployments of power that exist outside the law (1980b, 82–87). It is, as Foucault puts it, "poor in resources, sparing of its methods, monotonous in the tactics it utilizes, incapable of invention" (85). What is needed if we are to understand these new deployments of power is a political theory that is not erected around the problem of sovereignty: "[w]e need to cut off the king's head: in political theory that has still to be done" (1980c, 121). It is Foucault's aim to develop a theory of this new kind of power.

The most powerful metaphor that Foucault employs to describe this new kind of power is that of the "capillary": "But in thinking of the mechanisms of power, I am thinking rather of its capillary form of existence, the point where power reaches into the very grain of individuals, touches their bodies and inserts itself into their actions and attitudes, their discourse, learning processes and everyday lives" (39). He defines a number of characteristics that distinguish capillary power. First, it is everywhere—it is "'always already there,' that one is never 'outside' it" (141). It is coextensive with the social body; there are no spaces it does not encompass. Second, as a consequence of the pervasiveness of power, power relations are hidden from view, indeed, are "perhaps among the best hidden things in the social body" (1988a, 118).

One of the major differences between Foucault's theory of power and that of juridical power is that, for Foucault, power is productive rather than purely negative. Power produces knowledges, subjects, social relations (1980c, 59). Society is inconceivable without power. A society without power relations "can only be an abstraction" (1983b, 223). The juridical theory defined power as restrictive, oppressive, productive of nothing. Thus freedom or liberation was defined as the escape from or absence of power. But if power is everywhere, producing the very elements of social life, then freedom must be defined in different terms. Resistance to power cannot be, as in the juridical conception, escape from the power of the sovereign but, rather, an attempt to reconfigure power.

Rejecting the juridical sovereign also entails redefining power not as a thing but as a relation, a process. Power/domination is not one person dominating another, but, rather, a series of relations between and among people that extends through the social body, "a multiplicity of force relations immanent in the sphere in which they operate" (1980b, 92). Once more the capillary metaphor is useful. Capillaries are hard to trace. They are innumerable; they lack definable origin. In studying power we should not be looking for an origin—either in the state or the economy—but for the effects of power, the points of power that are manifest in relations (1980c, 96–97).

Foucault's injunction to cut off the king's head is central to his redefinition of power. But Foucault does not argue that the state and the apparatuses cre-

ated by it do not wield power. Rather he argues that sovereignty and disciplinary mechanisms "are absolutely integral constituents of the general mechanisms of power in society" (108). He is not claiming that no power resides in
the state, but that we must go beyond the power of the state to understand
modern power. The state, furthermore, occupies a unique place in the pantheon of power in society: it is the form of power that defines all the other
forms; it is the reference point for the other forms. Despite this, however, it
does not follow that these forms of power are derived from the state (1983b,
224). They have an independent existence that must be addressed in any attempt to understand—or change—that power.

The relationship between power in the state and beyond it is a complex aspect of Foucault's theory. Because state power defines the configuration of
power in the rest of society, a different configuration of state power will produce a different configuration of civil society. This is particularly important
for the contemporary situation of women in the United States. We live in a
state that permits much latitude in the institutions of civil society. It is also a
state that in most, but not all, respects has relinquished control of women's
sexuality. This is not true of all states. The position of women in the present-
day United States is a particular historical situation, not a general phenomenon. It dictates a particular, not a general, strategy.

Foucault's understanding of the nature of the relationship between state and
nonstate power is evident in one of the major subjects of his last works: what
he calls "governmentality." His discussion of this topic brings together the major themes of his theory of power. In a sense it is Foucault's effort to describe
the culmination and contemporary character of power. He defines *governing*
in the broadest sense as the effort to "structure the possible field of action of
others" (1983b, 221). Thus governmentality can encompass everything from
the government of oneself to the institutions of the administrative state. Governmentality for Foucault is, like disciplinary society, more an ethos than an
event. It describes a way of life in which everything, from the individual to the
state, is regimented, disciplined, and controlled (1991). This form of power,
Foucault claims, has become preeminent in the West: "We live in the era of
governmentality first discovered in the 18th century" (1991, 103). It also entails an understanding of the subject that is distinct from that of the juridical
subject. The juridical subject is a bearer of rights, the autonomous, rational
individual of the liberal/modernist tradition. The subject of governmentality,
in contrast, is a subject in relationship to others, a subject subjected to multiple forms of discipline, both state and nonstate (1988b, 20). "Power relations
are rooted in the system of social networks" (1983b, 224).

Even though Foucault's theory of power does not directly address the situation of women in the West, the implications for an analysis of women and power are profound. Lerner argues that the control of women's sexuality was a pillar of state power from its inception. For Foucault, a new form of power evolved in the West that, although it originated in state power, spread beyond the political/juridical into every aspect of society. This power is no longer localized in the state; it is in the very interstices of civil society. What this means for the effort to combat the subordination of women is, first, that we must develop an understanding of this non-state-based power and, second, that we must develop a new strategy of resistance in which the focus must shift from the state to the institutions and relations of society. Foucault's work on subjectification is instrumental in achieving both these objectives.

Subjectification and Resistance

Foucault's theories of power and subjectification are two sides of the same coin. His assertion that knowledge creates power and, particularly, power over subjects is the basis for his historical analyses of the prison, the asylum, the clinic, his more theoretical works, and his last works on the care of the self. The connection of power and subjectification encompasses the most challenging aspects of his approach. His thesis that the discourses he describes constitute subjects, that there is no essential subject prior to these discourses, is perhaps his most radical theoretical contribution. This thesis is inextricably connected to his equally radical claim that the contradiction inherent in the sciences of "man" places them in a unique position in the realm of knowledge. Finally, his theory of subjectification informs a theory of resistance that subverts the accepted definition of political resistance.

Foucault defines subjectification as "the procedure by which one obtains the constitution of a subject, or, more precisely, of a subjectivity which is of course only one of the given possibilities of organization of a self-consciousness" (1988a, 253). Each of Foucault's historical and theoretical works contributes to the development of this theory of subjectification. The historical analyses of the prison, asylum, and clinic illustrate how subjects are created by dividing practices. New categories of subjectivity are created where none existed before. Thus "the subject is objectified by a process of division either within himself or from others" (1983b, 208). These newly constituted subjects become the object, furthermore, of scientific classification. Discourses of knowledge are created about these subjects; institutions are created to discipline them in accordance with this knowledge; the sciences of man are institutionalized as mechanisms of control. Finally, Foucault examines how these discourses are internalized, how human beings turn themselves into subjects and govern themselves according to these discourses.

What Foucault proposes in his work is an analysis of subjectification "at the level of these continuous and ongoing processes which subject our bodies, govern our gestures, dictate our behaviors, etc." (1980c, 97). The implications of this theory are clear: his work constitutes the most thoroughgoing challenge to the autonomous subject of modernism. Foucault not only defines the individual as constituted by discourses, he also provides a concrete analysis of how that constitution functions. He looks at how bodies are disciplined by institutions and how individuals govern themselves in accordance with the discourses that create them as subjects. He examines how language/discourse quite literally sculpts bodies, even modifying organic processes (1965, 183).

Foucault's theory of subjectification is complex and wide ranging. Although Foucault does not explicitly discuss the identity "woman," feminists have found his work useful in exploring the constitution of this subject, and many contemporary feminist accounts of the social determination of "woman" are derived from Foucault's work. But as with any account of the social constitution of identity, Foucault must confront the problem of determinism. If we are all constituted and constrained by the discourses of our society, why are we not all the same, why do we not all become social dupes? Foucault's rejoinder to this criticism is his theory of resistance. An integral element of his theory of power is his assertion that "where there is power there is resistance" (1980b, 95). There is no relationship of power without the means of escape or flight (1983b, 225). Foucault argues that power is diffused throughout the social body, lacking a central point of origin. The same is true, he maintains, of resistance. "Points of resistance" are everywhere in power relations; there is no single locus of "great Refusal." Rather, points of resistance are mobile and transitory (1980b, 95–96). Resistance does not come from without but from within the power relation (1980c, 142).

One of the prevalent criticisms of a determinist stance is that it leads to quiescence. Foucault was particularly concerned to counter this charge: "My point is not that everything is bad, but that everything is dangerous, which is not the same thing. If everything is dangerous then we always have something to do. So my position leads not to apathy, but to a hyper- and pessimistic activism" (1983a, 231–32). But the kind of activism Foucault promotes is circumscribed by his theory of power. We cannot be liberated from power, because power is endemic to the social body. What we can do, however, is work to rearrange the structures of power in a more advantageous way, to develop "a new economy of power relations" (1983b, 210). What Foucault is arguing is that power and its concomitant restraints will always be part of the social body; society is inconceivable without power and knowledge. What we should ask is whether the particular system of restraints under which we live "leaves individuals the liberty to transform the system" (1988a, 294).

For Foucault, then, what we are resisting is not power per se but the particular configuration of power under which we live and the techniques of power that are employed in our society. Modern power structures are characterized by individualization and totalization; it is this that we must refuse: "[m]aybe the target nowadays is not to discover what we are, but to refuse what we are" (1983b, 216). We do this by promoting "new forms of subjectivity" (216). Our problem is not to liberate the individual from the state "but to liberate us both from the state and the type of individualization which is linked to the state. We have to promote new forms of subjectivity through the refusal of this kind of individuality which has been imposed on us for several centuries" (216). Where these new forms of subjectivity come from, however, poses a dilemma for Foucault. Since he has discarded the autonomous, constituting subject, he cannot posit subjects who discover their true selves. His alternative is vague. First, he suggests that certain experiences can lead to this creation. For example, he believes that the experience of sexuality can lead to a new experience of bodies and pleasures that resists the current deployment of sexuality (1980b, 157). Even less plausible is his argument that recent experiences with "drugs, sex, communes, other forms of consciousness, and other forms of individuality" can provide the "rough outline of a future society" (1977, 231). Second, he suggests that the alternative to the essential, constituting subject is the self as "a work of art" (1983a, 237), that is, the construction of the self from the available discourses.

Foucault's theory of subjectification and resistance is a bold departure. It jettisons the untenable presuppositions of the modernist subject and offers an alternative that explains the experience of subjectivity in contemporary society. The theory of resistance Foucault develops acknowledges the social constitution of identities and suggests a politics that reflects this fact. This is a key insight. Defining subjects as constituted by the myriad forces of society places the practice of identity politics in a new light. It makes it clear that what we are resisting in identity politics is not political power alone. Rather the object of resistance is the complex of discourses that is dispersed throughout society.

From the perspective I have developed in Chapter 3, what Foucault is talking about in his theory of subjectification and resistance is public identities. The "new forms of subjectivity" under which we are subsumed are the public

identities that are the object of identity politics. I have argued that resistance
to these public identities originates in personal identity, the core self that has
been formed by the experiences of each individual subject. Although these core
selves are profoundly influenced by the public identities that constrain us, each
core self is also constructed by unique social experiences. Without a core self
we would be unable to resist public identities.

Foucault does not take this tack. Like many critics of the autonomous subject of modernism, he refuses to discuss individual subjects and their unique
constitution. Since, like Butler, he assumes that any such discussion must presuppose the autonomous subject of modernism, he carefully avoids any reference to individuality. His theory of resistance suffers as a result. One way of
putting Foucault's dilemma is that his theory of resistance requires a subject
who acts, yet his theory of subjectification precludes such a subject. His solution is to sneak elements of the modernist subject in through the back door in
his theory of resistance. Foucault asserts that we have to create ourselves as a
work of art. Yet how can we conceive such a creative process without assuming an autonomous subject who does the creating, a subject who picks and
chooses from among the available options? He also urges that we judge power
structures on the basis of whether they offer us the "liberty to transform the
system" (1988a, 294). Liberty is a quality of the autonomous subject; it is incompatible with the constructed self that Foucault theorizes. And finally and
most definitively: "The critical ontology of ourselves has to be considered not
certainly, as a theory, a doctrine, nor even as a permanent body of knowledge
that is accumulating; it has to be conceived as an attitude, an ethos, a philosophical life in which the critique of what we are is at one and the same time
the historical analysis of the limits that are imposed on us and an experience
of the possibilities of going beyond them" (1984, 50).[2]

A key element of Foucault's theory of resistance is his blanket statement that
where there is power there is resistance. He offers no defense for this suppo-
sition. Nor does he offer an explanation for the fact that many people do not
resist the subjectification that society imposes on them. There is no room for
differentiation in Foucault's theory. For him we are all subjected to overwhelming forces that constitute us as subjects. But he then argues that far from
turning all of us into social dupes as one might expect, this power simultaneously produces points of resistance in all of us. Once more, this theory presupposes some form of the autonomous subject. It assumes that we will not all
turn into social dupes, because there is some deep source in all of us that causes
us to resist.

2. See Kruks 2001 for a compatible critique.

Throughout this book I have argued not that social determinist theories such as Foucault's are wrong but that they are incomplete. What Foucault's theory needs is, first, an understanding of the constitution of individual identities provided by object relations theory. Far from retreating to the modernist subject, object relations theory posits a subject that is wholly a social construct, but a particular social construct embedded in a particular social location. Second, Foucault's theory needs an understanding of the interaction between the personal identity that emerges from the child's social interactions and the public, hegemonic concepts that structure society. The hegemonic concepts of society do not wholly determine us. They are filtered through the particularities of the social situations of each individual. We need a theory that can explain that interaction.

Despite these lacunae in Foucault's theory, however, his work provides a valuable perspective for an understanding of identity politics. His work on power and subjectivity represents a significant departure for the human sciences. His theory of power forces us to look beyond the state to identify power structures in the contemporary world. Likewise, his theory of the creation of subjects through discourse provides us with an understanding of the subject that avoids the errors of the modernist subject and explains the constitution of subjectivity. Both these theories have profound implications for feminist theory and practice and, specifically, identity politics. In an era in which the regulation of sexuality is moving out of the governmental sphere, Foucault's theories focus our attention on nonstate power structures that create public identities. Foucault also provides us with tools to analyze the constitution of subjectivity and thus the means to resist it.

Although I want to build on these insights, I also want to push Foucault's theories further than he wants to go. His formulations offer a needed alternative to modernist theories, but he has not followed through on their radical potential. Foucault claims that power is everywhere, that it has moved beyond the state to the interstices of civil society. But in his actual analyses he concentrates heavily on the examination of state apparatuses. His discussions of the prison, the mental institution, governmentality—all focus on state or quasi-state organizations. Foucault's analysis of sexuality provides the best opportunity to realize the radical potential implicit in his approach. But even here Foucault never engages in a concrete analysis of how sexuality is constituted in civil society, in the practices of the family, in the influence of advertising, in economic practices, in religion. Foucault's theory defines these institutions as central to the practice of power, but he does not follow through by examining them fully. Engaging in such an examination would yield an even more radical perspective than that which he offers.

The Politics of Civil Society

In 1970 Kate Millett articulated a conviction that had informed feminist thought at least since the time of Wollstonecraft: sexual relations are political/power relations. In *Sexual Politics* Millett answered the question of whether the relationship between the sexes can be viewed as political with a resounding yes (1970, 23). "Coitus can scarcely be said to take place in a vacuum; although of itself it appears a biological and physical activity, it is set so deeply within the larger context of human affairs that it serves as a charged microcosm of the variety of attitudes and values to which culture subscribes" (23). Millett goes on to stress that it is opportune, even mandatory at this point to develop "a more relevant psychology and philosophy of power relationships beyond the simple conceptual framework provided by our traditional formal politics" (24). This new conception of power would be necessary for the "enormous social change" involved in a sexual revolution; what is required is "altered consciousness" (362). In sum, Millett calls for a cultural revolution that, while including political and economic reorganization, would go far beyond these boundaries (262).

That Millett's comments sound distinctly Foucaultian is not a coincidence. Although Millett lacks the theoretical sophistication of Foucault, that they arrive at the same theory is a function of the fact that they are asking a similar question. Both want to know how subjects are constituted in the contemporary world. Millett's question is particular: how is the subject "woman" constituted? Foucault's question is more general. But the question of the constitution of identity leads both to the conclusion that identities are constituted by the myriad forces that structure society. This conclusion, furthermore, leads them to another: we need a new theory of power to understand this constitution and, most important, a theory that moves beyond the political/legal sphere.

Millett is articulating a conviction that would become the defining principle of 1970s feminism: the personal is political. Although Millett is one of the first feminists to state this principle explicitly and forcefully, it came to be one of the central tenets of this wave of the feminist movement. From the 1960s onward, feminists realized that they were working for cultural, not solely political, change. The consciousness-raising movement of the 1960s and 1970s was the clearest expression of this conviction. Although feminists did not ignore political action, they defined changing cultural attitudes and social values as a central part of feminism. In other words, from the outset, feminists employed a dual strategy of both political and social/cultural activism.

Flash forward to the identity politics of the twentieth century. Things have changed significantly since Millett wrote *Sexual Politics*. Rereading her analysis thirty years later is instructive. Much of *Sexual Politics* is devoted to describing the condition of women in the United States in 1970. From a political, legal, and economic position, this condition has improved dramatically in thirty years. Much of the legal discrimination against women has been eradicated. Many more women, including married women with children, are in the workforce. Women hold jobs that were closed to them at the time that Millett wrote; they are legally guaranteed the same pay for these jobs as men receive. Politically, women have also scored significant successes. The women's vote has become a factor to reckon with in contemporary U.S. politics. Women have entered the political arena in ways that are remarkable from a 1970s perspective. If we look at the women's movement in terms of the other side of the dual strategy that Millett proposed, however, the report card is mixed. The social/cultural revolution that Millett called for has not been entirely successful. The public identity "woman" is still defined in ways that place women in an inferior position vis-à-vis men. The consciousness-raising that the 1970s feminists sought has only been partially accomplished.

The political and legal success of the women's movement is a stunning achievement. The fact that women have an accepted role in the political arena is a significant step forward in the evolution of the movement. The eradication of legal barriers is equally important. But this political and legal success has come at a price: it has to a certain extent obscured the importance of the social/cultural trajectory of the women's movement. Feminist identity politics is *politics*. It is focused on the political arena and defines problems in terms of political solutions. This has tended to overshadow what, for Millett and the 1970s feminists, was equally important: resistance in the social/cultural sphere. There is a certain irony to this development. The feminist movement's success in the political realm has meant that the number of issues facing feminists in the strictly political realm has decreased. Many of the political/legal battles have been fought and won. But this success has skewed the attention of the movement. Feminists' political success has inclined feminists to seek political solutions to every problem confronting feminism. Instead of turning increasingly to the social/cultural sphere, feminists have focused on the political sphere, the sphere of their significant triumphs.

What I am arguing, in other words, is that feminists have lost sight of the thesis advanced by Foucault and Millett. Power in the contemporary world is everywhere. Focusing almost exclusively on the political is not an effective strategy for change. It is time for the focus of the dual strategy of the feminist movement to shift from the political to the social. The forces that constrain and demean the public identity "woman" are not primarily political and legal. They are dispersed throughout the social body. Our resistance must be dispersed as well.

To illustrate this thesis, I will look at the controversy surrounding hate speech. Although this issue has been focused primarily on racist hate speech, the principles involved apply equally to the situation of women or any other marginalized group. Proponents of legislation against hate speech argue that this form of speech should not be legally protected because it is unique in the harm that it causes. One of the most effective arguments for legislation banning racist hate speech is in Mari Matsuda et al.'s *Words That Wound: Critical Race Theory, Assaultive, Speech, and the First Amendment* (1993). Matsuda argues that other nations, the United Kingdom, Canada, Australia, and New Zealand, have laws against racist hate speech and that the United States should follow suit. These laws, she asserts, function as effective protection of the civil liberties of the groups that are the object of this speech. In countries where racist hate speech is tolerated for "the good of society," we are asking subordinated groups to pay a great price, to sacrifice their civil liberties for the sake of freedom of speech (80).

Central to Matsuda's argument is her claim that racial insults are qualitatively different from other insults because they conjure up the entire history of racial discrimination (100). But her argument for legislation banning such speech has an important proviso: it does not cover racist speech originating in the subordinated groups. This speech, she argues, must be interpreted as the victims' struggle for self-identity in response to racism. Unlike the racist speech of the dominant group, this speech is not tied to the structural domination of another group. The harm of the kind of racist speech she seeks to outlaw is that it works in concert with other racist tools to keep victims in an inferior position (39).

As this significant proviso indicates, Matsuda does not claim that fighting racist hate speech through legislation will be easy. Racism is ubiquitous. It is mostly unconscious; it is so woven into our culture that it appears normal (77). She concludes: "I believe that the speech/acts that 'race' us must all be fought simultaneously, for they are mutually dependent parts of a whole" (83). But although she concedes that the problem of racism that the legislation against racist speech seeks to address is extralegal, she nevertheless argues that we should seek a legal remedy. Ultimately she asserts that we can solve the problem of racist hate speech with what she calls "legal imagination" (50).

The arguments against hate speech legislation focus primarily on the point that Matsuda concedes here, the complexity of the phenomenon of racism. Although hardly typical of these arguments, Judith Butler's position emphasizes this complexity. Butler's *Excitable Speech: A Politics of the Performative* (1997a) is a direct reply to Matsuda's argument in *Words That Wound*. Butler begins her analysis of the problem posed by hate speech with a general question: "When we claim to have been injured by language, what kind of claim do we make?" (1) Her answer is that the claim of injury entails ascribing an agency to language. It follows that we exercise the force of language even as we seek to counter that force. No act of censorship can undo that force. This general thesis about the role of language in social life is the basis of Butler's claim that hate speech legislation must necessarily be ineffective.

What Butler attempts to accomplish in *Excitable Speech* is to complicate the issues that surround the debate over legislation to curb hate speech. She begins by questioning what it means to be called a name. Naming is one of the first forms of "linguistic injury" that we encounter as individuals. But, Butler continues, all name-calling is not injurious. Names create the possibility of social life; language calls us into social existence. Naming can derogate and demean, but naming in general is what social existence is all about; it is unavoidable (2–5).

Butler then turns to the specific kind of naming that characterizes hate speech. Threats require certain kinds of circumstances and a venue of power in which the effects of the threat can be realized (12). To understand how a threat can be effective as a threat, more than the words must be analyzed. It is the context in which the threat is spoken that constitutes it as a threat. Complicating matters further is the fact that words which in certain circumstances are injurious can be revalued by the intended recipients of the injury and become vehicles of resistance. The revaluation of *queer* is a particularly apt example of this phenomenon. In certain circumstances, *queer* is intended to be and is an insult. Used by the gay and lesbian community, however, it is a means of resistance to hegemonic power and a strategy to transform a demeaned public identity (13).

Although this argument alone would seem to end the debate over the viability of hate speech legislation, this is only the beginning of Butler's analysis. Her subsequent argument turns on the thesis that informs her work in *Gender Trouble* as well: subjects are constituted in language. This "primary vulnerability" to language characterizes the social role of language. It follows that it is impossible to effectively regulate the potentially injurious effects of language without destroying this fundamental characteristic of language itself (1997a, 26–30). Butler then goes on to analyze another aspect of hate speech that militates against effective legislation. The speaker of hate speech does not originate the speech that he/she employs. Rather, it is the social context of the speech that gives it force. As even Matsuda concedes, the effect of hate speech depends on the history of racial discrimination. But how do we prosecute this history? The speaker of hate speech is not solely responsible for this history, yet the effectiveness of the speech depends on its existence. As Butler puts it, the speaker of a racist slur is making linguistic community with a history of speakers (52). There is even the possibility that prohibiting hate speech, and thus calling attention to it, might actually increase its power to wound (38).

Butler brings all these arguments together in an explicitly Foucaultian context. Like Foucault, she puts the question, If power is no longer located in sovereignty, how can we locate the source of hate speech's injury? The law forces us to locate the injury of hate speech in a particular subject addressed to another subject. What this misses, however, is what Butler calls the "sedimentation of power in practices." Racist speech does not originate with the subject, but is embedded in the social structure; it is this structure that gives it efficacy (78–80). But it is precisely this structure that is immune to legislation.

My argument concerning the role of public identities has much in common with the position that Butler espouses in *Excitable Speech*. We are both arguing that what I call public identities are a common and unavoidable aspect of social life. They constitute and in some cases demean the identities of individuals in any given society. Where we part company is that Butler assumes that this social construction is the only element constituting identity. I have argued that individuals have both personal and public identities and that it is in the interface of these two identities that resistance takes place.

Despite this difference, however, I entirely agree with Butler's Foucaultian rejection of legislation against hate speech. The push to ban hate speech is an excellent example of the tendency I am criticizing: the assumption that all problems have a political/legal solution. The structure of identity politics in the present-day United States inclines its participants to turn to the law to rectify social ills. The virtue of Butler's account is that she effectively demonstrates that the problem of hate speech is embedded in myriad aspects of the social structure; it is historical, linguistic, and pervasive. The remedy for hate speech is social, not political. The phenomenon is too complex to legislate away; attempts to do so may very well make the situation worse rather than better.

Another particularly pointed example of the issue I am raising is Catharine MacKinnon's advocacy of an injunction that defines pornography as a civil offense against women. Like the proponents of legislation against hate speech, MacKinnon attempts to solve the complex social problems manifest in pornography in the legal sphere. Legislation against hate speech defines it as the action of a single subject against another subject. Likewise, MacKinnon's injunction defines pornography as the act of a single pornographer against the civil rights of a single woman. That this characterization misrepresents the phenomenon of pornography in our society is clear to those on both sides of this issue. The problem of pornography, like that of racist hate speech, is deeply embedded in our institutions and practices. It is significant that one of MacKinnon's arguments is that acts of racism that parallel the sexism in pornography are not tolerated in our society. What she fails to note, however, is that this is not the case because racist acts have been made illegal, but, rather, because social attitudes toward race have changed. Attitudes toward sexism must change before pornography is eradicated. Legal remedies are not the appropriate means to effect this transformation.

To be fair to MacKinnon, however, she is fully aware of this contradiction. From her perspective the fact that our legal system forces us to define injury in terms of one individual acting on another is the principal liability of that system. Her defense of the injunction is that we have to use the tools available to us, in this case the existing legal system, to accomplish our ends. This is a persuasive argument, but ultimately it does not address the problems raised by Butler and Foucault. If anything, it reveals, once again, why a legal remedy is inappropriate.

What I am arguing, then, is not that the participants in identity politics should ignore the state and downplay the significant gains that they have made in the political arena. Rather, I am arguing that feminists in particular and the participants in identity politics in general should adopt a Foucaultian strategy of resistance. This strategy entails an understanding of power that recognizes its scope. Power is everywhere. Resisting power only in the political/legal sphere is not an effective strategy in contemporary Western society. We need a dual strategy that simultaneously targets the social and political, a strategy that recognizes the capillary nature of power and its functioning in society. We must move beyond the assumption that every problem has a political solution.

Foucault's argument that we need to cut off the king's head, that we need a new theory of power to explain contemporary society, has not transformed the discipline of political theory. As the discussion of liberalism in Chapter 2 indicates, contemporary political theory in the United States is still focused primarily on the strictly political sphere. There is a significant exception to this characterization, however. In recent years a number of political theorists have turned their attention to a subject that has distinctly Foucaultian overtones: civil society. The contemporary analysis of civil society by at least some political theorists is an implicit acknowledgment that power is not limited to the political sphere but is rather, as Foucault argues, dispersed throughout society.

The best example of this attitude is the comprehensive analysis of civil society and political theory by Jean Cohen and Andrew Arato. Cohen and Arato define civil society as "the sphere of social interaction between economy and state, composed above all of the intimate sphere (especially the family), the sphere of associations (especially voluntary associations), social movements and forms of public communication" (1992, ix). It is significant that Cohen and Arato define Foucault's work as central to the analysis of civil society. They argue that Foucault shifts the emphasis of political theory from the state to the categories of civil society. In an extensive and generally favorable analysis of Foucault's work, Cohen and Arato argue that he effectively replaces the juridical concept of power with a "strategic model of hostile, asymmetrical relation of forces" (266). They even concede that it is possible to construct a civil society-based strategy of resistance on the basis of Foucault's theory (292). Despite this concession, however, the Habermasian perspective that Cohen and Arato adopt leads them to a fundamental criticism of Foucault's approach: his work lacks the normative dimension they are seeking in their analysis.

Cohen and Arato's analysis makes it clear that they see the study of civil society as effectively transforming the discipline of political theory. As they note, the realm of civil society is where most people in modern society spend the majority of their time (170). Following Hegel, they argue that civil society constitutes the ethical life of the subjects of contemporary societies. Like Foucault, Cohen and Arato realize that the analysis of civil society entails a different strategy of resistance from that dictated by the juridical conception of power. In a significant claim, they argue that the women's movement identified the importance of civil society from the outset. They point out that feminists have always recognized that socially constructed conventional gender identities preserved male privilege and worked against women's autonomy and self-determination. Consequently, the feminist movement adopted a dualistic strategy targeting both state and civil society (551).

It would be premature to conclude, however, that all or even most contemporary political theorists have adopted a Foucaultian attitude toward civil society. To a certain extent, this is to be expected. Political theorists, by definition, study politics, a realm that, since Aristotle, has been defined in opposition to the private sphere. Challenging this opposition, as Foucault clearly realizes, changes everything. Cutting off the king's head means that political theorists analyze not just politics, but all manifestations of power in society. This is not a change that will happen overnight.

Two recent books on civil society and political theory illustrate the ways in which political theorists have attempted to deal with this challenge. In neither case has the attempt been successful. The first, an edited volume titled *Civil Society and Government* (Rosenblum and Post 2002) takes a very different tack from that of Cohen and Arato. In their introduction to the volume, the editors define the difference between civil society and government as that between the particular and the universal: "In contrast to the pluralism and particularism of civil society, government may be defined as standing for inclusive public norms and common identity. Through an overarching public political culture embodied in institutions and perpetuated through many forms of public education, direct and indirect, government articulates and sustains shared ground. It claims authoritatively to represent common interests" (Post and Rosenblum 2002, 8–9). Post and Rosenblum are careful to follow this statement with a disclaimer that this vision of the common good is always "somebody's vision." But it is clear from the essays they collect in the volume that from their perspective the analysis of civil society, far from transforming the discipline of political theory, fits neatly under the rubric of *liberal political theory*. There is, as one might expect, no discussion of a Foucaultian perspective on civil society. Nor is there any suggestion that civil society may exert coercive power over citizens. As far as Post and Rosenblum are concerned, government necessarily sets the rules for civil society and, therefore, by definition, continues to be the single locus of power in society.

The second book, Jodi Dean's edited volume, *Cultural Studies and Political Theory: Feminism After Identity* (2000), fails to meet the challenge of civil society in a very different sense. Most of the essays either criticize the political as ideological or fault cultural studies for not being sufficiently political. While the Rosenblum and Post work stays solidly within the ideology of liberal political theory, Dean's collection moves into a wholly new ideological terrain. The authors' definition of this terrain, however, does not fulfill the promise of the volume's title. The analyses in the book are not, strictly speaking, analyses of power. The book contains no sustained analysis of the operation of power in civil society and how this might be incorporated into political theory. It is just such an analysis, however, that is required if we are to cut off the king's head in political theory.[3]

Foucault calls for a new conception of power that would enable us to understand and resist domination in the contemporary world. Analysts of civil society such as Cohen and Arato reinforce this argument by locating power outside the strictly legal/political sphere. The feminist movement has embraced this insight from the outset, calling for consciousness-raising and the transformation of social values in addition to political action. It is my belief that we

---

3. Anne Norton's *Republic of Signs* (1993) presents a unique case for my analysis. Norton concurs that power is everywhere is society; the power of liberal political ideology is replicated in many aspects of society. Although this is an intriguing analysis, it ignores Foucault's point that power in society is independent of that of the state.

must not lose sight of this insight; we must act on what we already know. Feminist identity "politics" must operate primarily outside the boundaries of politics. It must be about contesting the constitution of identities in the sphere of civil society. This calls for a different theory and practice from that embraced by most contemporary feminist identity politics.

The work of Iris Marion Young illustrates the practices of feminist identity politics that I am contesting. Even though the focus of Young's work is difference and the effects of difference throughout society, in *Justice and the Politics of Difference* she concentrates her attention exclusively on the public sphere. "Justice" is political justice. It is defined and enacted exclusively in the political arena. The "politics of difference" she argues for is likewise exclusively political. No attention is given to how the identities that make up these political groups are constituted or where that constitution takes place. When Young does mention civil society in *Inclusion and Democracy* (2000), it is to dismiss it. Civil society, she argues, is *not* a preferred alternative to the state for promoting democracy and social justice. She concludes that civil society can only minimally advance values of self-development (156).

Although the exclusively political focus of Young characterizes most feminist identity politics, feminists in disciplines outside political theory have embraced a viewpoint more consistent with the approach I am advocating. Feminist work in philosophy, psychology, anthropology, and many other disciplines has documented how identities are constituted by the diverse array of forces that make up civil society. These studies have led at least some feminist political theorists to turn to civil society as the source of resistance to the subordination of women. Kirstie McClure, for example, argues that the state is no longer the privileged location of political address. In the modern world, she asserts, new political spaces have emerged, a "diffusion of political sites across the surface of the social itself" (1992, 123). Jodi Dean's analysis in *The Solidarity of Strangers* (1996) also focuses on civil society. Dean argues that civil society no longer represents a division between the public and private spheres, but, rather, a multiplicity of differing spheres (97).[4] These voices, however, are far from predominant in the discipline of political theory.

Perhaps the clearest instance of theorists who adopt a Foucaultian perspective on power are commentators on the constitution of racism in our society. The discussion of racist hate speech has focused on the complexity of racism in our society. This has led many theorists of race to argue that the law is an inappropriate instrument to combat not only racist hate speech but racism in general. For Charles Lawrence, for example, racism is transmitted as a value

---

4. See also Rose 1996 for a strategy of resistance that moves beyond the political.

in our culture. Thus even without conscious intent, racist actions can occur. Lawrence draws the implication of this for the law: "[T]he existing intent requirements' assignment of individual fault as responsibility for the existence of racial discrimination distorts our perceptions about the causes of discrimination and leads us to think about racism in a way that advances the disease rather than combating it" (1995, 239). Lawrence argues that by insisting on a blameworthy perpetrator, the Supreme Court's ruling creates an imaginary world that does not exist. As he puts it, "We cannot be individually blamed for unconsciously harboring attitudes that are inescapable in a culture permeated with racism" (239).

Lawrie Balflour's discussion of "race consciousness" is informed by a similar conviction. Balflour argues that race consciousness provides a way of capturing those effects of racial identity that are untouched by the idea of racial discrimination, understood as a category of discrete acts. It can explain how, in our society, racial hierarchy is simultaneously condemned and taken for granted (1998, 347). Patricia Williams's well-known discussions of racism also echo these beliefs. Williams defines racial discrimination as "so pervasive, yet so hard to prosecute, so active yet so unactionable" (1997, 230). Williams has even coined a term for the negative effects of racial discrimination on identity: "spirit-murder." Spirit-murder, is a disregard for others whose lives qualitatively depend on our regard; the result is social structures that produce fear and hate (234).

Despite these convictions, however, Williams's work also provides an example of the prejudice toward the political that I am criticizing. Williams is not content to leave her analysis with the claim that racism is pervasive and insidious: "I think we need to elevate what I call spirit-murder to the conceptual, if not punitive level of a capital moral offense. We need to see it as cultural cancer; we need to open our eyes to the spiritual genocide it is wreaking on blacks, whites and the abandoned and abused of all races and ages. We need to eradicate its numbing pathology before it wipes out what precious little humanity we have left" (234). Exactly what Williams means by this is unclear. Perhaps her tendencies as a lawyer so strongly incline her to legal action that she cannot resist the temptation to move her argument into legal territory. But her very characterization of the phenomenon of racism as "spirit-murder" reveals the absurdity and futility of turning to the law to eradicate its effects. By the terms of her own analysis, a "cultural cancer" is not susceptible to legal remedy.

Sexism, like racism, is a cultural cancer. It cannot be eradicated by passing yet one more law banning sexual discrimination. Like racism, it goes deeper than individual acts by particular people. Its societal roots have to be addressed by extralegal means. I should make it clear, however, that in suggesting a politics of civil society I am not arguing that we should entirely ignore the state. Rather, following Foucault, I am urging that we see the state in its relationship to civil society. In his discussion of power in contemporary society, Foucault maintains both that we need a new theory of power that recognizes the nonstate forces that constitute power and that the state establishes the parameters of these forces. Thus his theory of power does not so much ignore the state as decenter it. A theory that seeks to explain the powers that constitute identity in contemporary society must include an analysis of the state in which the role of the state is recognized as a kind of framing mechanism for civil society. The nature and character of the state establish the boundaries and extent of the powers in civil society, powers that, in our particular society, are both pervasive and independent.

The interface of state and nonstate power over the constitution of identities is not a common topic among political theorists. One exception is Drucilla Cornell. In *The Imaginary Domain* (1995) Cornell argues that we must protect, as a legal matter of equality, "the equivalent bases for the chance to transform ourselves into the individuated being we think of as persons" (5). Central to this project, for Cornell, is imagination, the ability to imagine oneself as a person. What she calls the "imaginary domain" is crucial to the very possibility of freedom. One of the principal aspects of personhood constituted in the imaginary domain is our sense of ourselves as sexuate beings. Thus to deny a person his/her life as a sexuate being is to deny a fundamental part of identity (8). Individuation is "an extremely fragile achievement, one made possible by spinning out a meaning for an image of a coherent self from a pre-given web of social ties, symbolic relations, and primordial identifications" (38). For Cornell, political and legal philosophy do not give free weight to this social and symbolic constitution of the self. Although this relational and symbolic constitution of the self has no necessary political and legal conclusions, it does demand that we protect the legal conditions under which individuation is achieved and maintained. The state and legal system are symbolic Others that confirm and constitute who is established as a person (43).

What emerges from Cornell's analysis is a theory in which state and nonstate power conjointly constitute the identity "woman." On the one hand, she concedes that the law can only play a limited role in the regulation of imagistic signifiers. Yet she asserts on the other hand that feminists must change the "general grammar of culture" and that the law is a key part of that culture: "We should not demand that we *be* as women before the law; we should demand instead equivalent evaluation by the law of our sexual difference" (236).

I want to emphasize and endorse two aspects of Cornell's approach. First, although her focus is the law, Cornell makes it clear that the transformation she envisions goes far beyond the political and legal sphere. It is in the "grammar of culture" that change will take place; law is a part of this grammar but not its entirety. Second, and most significant, even the legal transformation that Cornell is seeking does not entail changing existing laws. Her argument is that we must change the concept of "person" that is implicit in legal opinions. This change is much more difficult to effect than enacting new laws. It entails changing judges' attitudes, the assumptions that inform the opinions they write. Although this change would be reflected in legal opinions, it could only be accomplished by extralegal means. Judges are people living in society. Their attitudes toward women, attitudes that will be reflected in their legal opinions, will be affected by changes in societal attitudes. Those attitudes are not subject to legislative fiat.

My argument, then, is that we need a dual strategy of resistance if we are to change identities in the contemporary world. The state and legal system must be one part of this strategy. The concept of "person" that informs the law has a profound effect on the status of women in our society. This was my thesis in Chapter 2. But in order to change that concept, we must keep several things in mind. This concept is embedded in the grammar of culture that extends far beyond the political/legal sphere. Further, even within the law, the concept of "person" is not most effectively altered by legislative initiative. Judges with a different conception of "person," one that recognizes difference and embodiment, will render legal opinions quite different from those that are based on the concept of the neutral, abstract citizen. Producing these judges by changing the society that informs their opinions, not legislative action, should be the focus of our strategy of resistance.

Conclusion: Recognizing Difference

Object relations theory urges us to see identity as a complexly constituted social product. We are social beings but not social dupes. We possess core selves but these selves are not the essential, neutral, autonomous selves of modernism. It has been the thesis of this book that bringing the social, relational self of object relations theory into the public, political realm creates a radically different politics. Tearing the veil from the abstract, neutral citizen of liberalism transforms that polity, creating a politics in which identities are recognized and legitimated. Differences between identities become the starting point of politics rather than that which must be eliminated.

I have argued that this new politics of identity must embrace a dual strategy of both political and social/cultural resistance. In conclusion I want to explicate what is entailed by each aspect of this strategy. In this chapter I have focused on the work of Foucault with the aim of outlining a strategy of resistance that targets the sources of power dispersed throughout society. One of the best illustrations of this new "politics" is an incident related by Jodi Dean in her book on the possibility of a postidentity feminist politics. On July 33, 1994, the *New York Times* reported that in the city of Billings, Montana, the Ku Klux Klan had engaged in a series of acts of racism, homophobia, and anti-Semitism. Among these was an incident in which a cinder block was thrown through a child's menorah-decorated window. In protest, several thousand non-Jewish families decorated their homes with menorahs, effectively negating the Klan's action (Dean 1996, 180). The people of Billings could have employed a legal strategy against the Klan. Smashing the window was, after all, an illegal act. Police protection for Jewish homes could have been instituted. But what the people of Billings did instead was more effective. It was a form of resistance to violence and intimidation that dealt with the problem where it originated: in societal values.

This example is dramatic and perhaps unique. But the strategy of resistance informing the action is significant. It is a strategy that has come to the forefront in recent decades. What Hilde Lindemann Nelson (2001) calls "damaged identities" have increasingly sought repair in the social rather than the political sphere. This has been particularly true in the women's movement. One of the criticisms of third wave feminism by second wavers has been that they are not sufficiently political. I think this criticism is misplaced. The third wave's emphasis on the social rather than the political is an appropriate strategy in contemporary society. The Riot Grrrls and the Girlie Movement are striking at the heart of problems that women face today. Their strategies, which only sometimes encompass political action, are suited to the nature of the power they confront. Foucault is right: we need a new theory of power and a new practice of resistance to combat this phenomenon that characterizes contemporary society. I do not think this thesis has been fully embraced either by contemporary feminist theorists or by theorists of identity politics.

It should be evident from the foregoing discussion that the political aspect of the dual strategy I am advocating is anything but straightforward. Most of the advocates of the politics of difference/identity discussed above have argued for a reform of the liberal polity that institutionalizes group participation. Iris Marion Young, in particular, is a strong proponent of this position. My problem with this approach is that it results in the fixing of identity that is the Achilles heel of identity politics. In Chapter 3, I argued that many of these problems could be avoided by focusing on the distinction between public and personal identities. This perspective yields another vision of the politics of difference. This vision is based on the understanding that we participate in group/identity politics because we identify with the goals of a particular group. This identification is not predetermined but is, rather, the function of a complex mix of issues surrounding the public identity that the group defines and the private identities of the individuals who participate in the group, which, in turn, are shaped by public identities. Assigning individuals to objectively determined structurally disadvantaged groups violates this understanding. Fixing these groups as permanent elements of government administration does so as well. In short, a politics that entails fixing the identities of citizens and fixing group identities in politics is not a useful model for identity politics.

One could argue, however, that defining certain groups as structurally disadvantaged is, at this point in U.S. history, both obvious and necessary. Certain groups *are* structurally disadvantaged; institutionalizing their participation is an attempt to overcome this disadvantage. The problem with this position, however, is that it presupposes that membership in one of these structurally disadvantaged groups overrides all other aspects of identity. It is not an identity I choose but one I am assigned. Thus my representation as, for example, an African American is fixed in the political system because of the historically structurally disadvantaged position of this group in U.S. society. This presumes too much. As an African American I may in most cases identify primarily with this aspect of my identity. I may embrace African American identity politics and espouse the goals of this movement. But this identification will not necessarily occur in every case. It is possible that I may identify primarily with some other aspect of my identity—my labor union membership or my status as a middle-class professional. In this case it would be inappropriate to fix my political representation solely in terms of racial identity.

The point I am making here is informed by Minow's assertion that we should replace a politics of "I am" for one of "I want." Although in many, perhaps most, cases what I want politically as an African American will be related to my racial identity. But to assume that this will always be the case is to return to an essentialist conception of identity. African American citizens should not be compelled to be classified by their race for political purposes. If they choose to do so, they should have that opportunity. But the impetus for identity politics must come from the participants themselves. Forcing citizens into preordained groups will not accomplish the objective of bringing identity into the political arena. Citizens will identify with particular groups out of a desire to achieve certain objectives. In the present political climate those objectives will in many, perhaps even most, cases, be related to challenging a hegemonic identity. But the impetus for such political action must be "I want" this objective, not "I am" this identity in an essentialist sense.

I want to attach two caveats to this proposal. First, it does not entail a return to the rational, autonomous chooser of the liberal tradition. The individual who chooses an identity group does so out of a complex mix of social forces that incline her to identify with this particular group. Those forces will incline some women, for example, to choose feminist politics, others not. Assigning all women the same identity and thus the same identity politics violates the differences between women just as surely as the concept "citizen" did under liberalism. Identifying with a group for a particular political purpose brings an aspect of an individual's identity into the public arena; it does not, as in liberal politics, deny that identity.

My second caveat is that although what I am advocating here sounds very much like the coalition politics that has become very popular among feminists and other advocates of the politics of difference, it differs in important ways from that politics. Coalition politics seems to solve many of the problems posed by identity politics. While identity politics is fragmenting, dividing us in society, coalition politics brings us together. In coalitions, members of a variety of identity groups come together under a common rubric. The advantage of coalition politics is that it retains difference while accomplishing commonality. Different identities are united for a common purpose without relinquishing those identities.

In one sense, coalition politics seems to be the perfect embodiment of Minow's politics of "I want." It envisions different identity groups coming together into a coalition for a particular purpose. Thus Hispanics, African Americans, feminists, and others might unite to accomplish a particular objective, the defense of affirmative action, for example. Each group would retain its uniqueness and difference. The coalition would not erase difference but be built on it. Furthermore, the unity of the coalition would be to achieve *this* particular objective. The participants in the coalition would not assume that the coalition would extend indefinitely. On the contrary, another coalition involving a different array of identity groups might form to achieve a different political objective.

Audre Lorde once stated, "As a 49–year-old Black lesbian feminist socialist mother of two including one boy, and a member of an interracial couple, I usually find myself part of some group defined as other, deviant, inferior, or just plain wrong" (1984, 114). In a coalition politics based on Minow's principle of "I want," Lorde could and would move freely from one identity group to another depending on the issue at hand. Thus she might identify as a lesbian to combat discrimination against gays and lesbians, as an African American to fight racial discrimination, and as a feminist to achieve rights for women. None of the aspects of her identity would be denied. Ideally, coalition politics would entail an acknowledgment of the complexity of individual identities and facilitate movement from one group to another as political issues dictate.

In practice, however, coalition politics does not work out this way. The defenders of coalition politics define it as a tool to combat complex systems of oppression and privilege. But implicit in this defense is the assumption that the identities of the groups constituting the coalition are fixed. Each group represents an aspect of oppression. The logic of coalition politics is based on the assumption that each group composing the coalition represents a partial perspective on oppression and that, together, these groups can fight oppression as a whole.[5] But nowhere in this vision is there a recognition that individuals will move from one identity group to another depending on the issue at hand. Nor is there a recognition that, as in Lorde's case, different oppressions would converge on a single individual. Rather, the advocates of coalition politics assume that individuals have a particular place in oppressive institutions, and it is from this *one* place that they enter first identity politics and then coalition politics. Audre Lorde must *choose* her oppression. She is not free to move from one group to another as issues demand.[6] Thus coalition politics as it is currently practiced perpetuates the fixing of identities that mars contemporary identity politics. It does not facilitate identification as the basis for political action.

Like many of the advocates of identity politics, I envision a politics in which particular identities are welcome and recognized. It is a politics that jettisons the identity of the abstract, universal citizen and replaces it with an embodied citizen who brings the particularities of her identity into the political arena. Unlike many of these advocates, however, I do not think this should be accomplished by fixing identities in the political system. We cannot assume which citizens will identify with which identities on which political issues. This should be a matter of choice based on the complexities of personal identities and individuals' particular relationships to public identities. It should not be a matter of government fiat. The model we should espouse here is Minow's, not Young's. Citizens will identify with the goals of particular identity groups

---

5. For a defense of coalition politics along these lines, see Fowlkes 1997.

6. Gloria Anzaldúa's (1987) discussion of the "new *mestiza*" is, I think, congruent with the version of coalition politics I am espousing here. For Anzaldúa, the *mestiza* consciousness breaks down paradigms, straddles two or more cultures; it requires developing a tolerance for contradictions and ambiguity.

to accomplish particular political purposes. Neither this identity nor this identification should be fixed.

I have argued throughout this book that the transformation of the liberal polity I am advocating entails a radically different understanding of citizenship and political action. Challenging these concepts challenges the foundation of our political system. Impartiality, the rule of the abstract citizen, are at the center of our legal and political understandings. The picture that holds us captive dictates a blindfold justice, the rejection of identity in the political sphere. Many of the legal reforms of recent decades have been efforts to change these conceptions, to reveal, for example, the masculinity of the law. These efforts have been successful up to a point. They have eradicated much of the overt discrimination in the law. Changing the picture that holds us captive is now a different kind of problem. Changing the picture at this point in time in the United States does not entail extensive constitutional or legal change. It entails a change in focus and attitude, not a change in law and constitution. We have changed laws and politics. Now we must change the attitudes that created those laws and politics.

I am not optimistic that this change will occur overnight. But in conclusion I would like to point to some aspects of our political and legal system that seem to indicate that some of the elements of the picture are starting to change. Take politics. We already live in an era in which identity politics is an accepted aspect of our political system. As Nathan Glazer says, we are all multiculturalists now. We already have a multicultural polity; what we lack is a full acceptance of that polity. Identity politics is still the realm of the "other." "Normal" citizens do not have an identity, only the "others" do. What we need to change is our attitudes toward identity. We need an acceptance of the embodied citizen, a polity in which identity is not suspect but required. This requires attitudinal, not structural, change.

The same situation characterizes the legal system. Feminist and critical legal theorists are pushing us in the direction of an acknowledgment of difference. The discretion in our legal system allows judges and juries to tailor their decisions to the particularities of individual cases. Concepts are entering the law that pull us away from the universal legal subject and bring difference in as a legitimate aspect of adjudication. The introduction of the concept of the "reasonable woman" discussed in Chapter 2 is an indication of this change. Although this standard still begs the question of the differences between women, it is a movement in the direction of difference. A number of legal theorists, furthermore, are arguing that the legal system has begun to accept a more complex understanding of the subject in the law. The pregnant woman, the battered wife, the sexually harassed employee are all new to the legal scene.

Others will follow. The legal system has and will continue to accommodate this complexity.[7]

What these changes suggest is that difference is beginning to move into our legal and political system, albeit slowly. These changes point to a system in which difference is regarded as the place to start rather than a danger to be avoided. What if, instead of resolving political or legal conflicts by looking first to a universal standard, we looked rather to the unique characteristics of the situation? Thus instead of agonizing over what general category covers the case of pregnant women, we would assume instead that this is a unique condition that requires a unique judicial and legal approach. What if, instead of assuming that every minority group within the United States must be subsumed under the same policy, we rather assumed that each has a unique history and each must be approached, legally and politically, from the perspective of that history? And, most pointed, what if we assumed that the position of women in our legal and political system calls for a set of policies that recognizes and speaks to the distinctive roles that a wide variety of women have assumed in that system?[8]

In his discussion of modern constitutionalism, Tully argues that the rejection of the "ancient" constitution that was based on tradition and custom transformed our political universe. The replacement of a hierarchy of statuses with the promise of a realm of universality and impartially paved the way for a new political order. The advantage of this new order is that it established the principles of equality and justice for all as the cornerstone of political order. This is an invaluable contribution. No one is suggesting that we abandon these principles. What we have not acknowledged, however, is that in practice inequality and hierarchy have been reestablished by the political order that sought to abolish them. But this time the inequality and hierarchy are not visible because they are hidden behind the veil of the universal citizen. It is time to tear away the veil, to acknowledge difference and identity and make them work to our advantage, to take the risk of difference.

7. See Boyle 1991 and Abrams 1994 for discussions of this complexity. Some legal theorists have even argued that the law is changing faster than societal values (Fineman 1995).

8. It is significant that the contemporary concern of many leftists is how to reconceive the universal in the face of the demise of Marxism (Butler, Laclau, and Žižek 2000).

BIBLIOGRAPHY

Abrams, Kathryn. 1994. "Title VII and the Complex Female Subject." *Michigan Law Review* 92 (8): 2479–540.

Alcoff, Linda. 1988. "Cultural Feminism Versus Post-Structuralism: The Identity Crisis in Feminist Theory." *Signs* 13 (3): 405–36.

Anzaldúa, Gloria. 1987. *Borderlands/La Frontera: The New Mestiza*. San Francisco: Aunt Lute.

Aronowitz, Stanley. 1995. "Reflections on Identity." In *The Identity in Question*, ed. John Rajchman, 111–27. New York: Routledge.

Balflour, Lawrie. 1998. "'A Most Disagreeable Mirror': Race Consciousness as Double Consciousness." *Political Theory* 26 (3): 346–69.

Barry, Brian. 2001. *Culture and Equality: An Egalitarian Critique of Multiculturalism*. Cambridge: Harvard University Press.

Baumeister, Andrea. 2000. *Liberalism and the Politics of Difference*. Edinburgh: Edinburgh University Press.

Benhabib, Seyla. 1992. *Situating the Self: Gender, Community, and Postmodernism in Contemporary Ethics*. New York: Routledge.

———. 1999. "Sexual Difference and Collective Identities: The New Global Constellation." *Signs* 24 (2): 335–61.

Bickford, Susan. 1996. *The Dissonance of Democracy: Listening, Conflict, and Citizenship*. Ithaca: Cornell University Press.

———. 1997. "Anti-anti-identity Politics: Feminism, Democracy, and the Complexities of Citizenship." *Hypatia* 12 (4): 111–31.

———. 1999. "Reconfiguring Pluralism: Identity and Institutions in the Inegalitarian Polity." *American Journal of Political Science* 43 (1): 88–108.

Bowlby, John. 1988. *A Secure Base: Parent-Child Attachment and Healthy Human Development*. New York: Basic Books.

Boyle, James. 1991. "Is Subjectivity Possible? The Post Modern Subject in Legal Theory." *University of Colorado Law Review* 62 (91): 489–524.

Brennan, Teresa, and Carole Pateman. 1979. "'Mere Auxiliaries to the Commonwealth: Women and the Origins of Liberalism.'" *Political Studies* 27 (2): 183–200.

Brown, Lyn Mikel, and Carol Gilligan. 1992. *Meeting at the Crossroads: Women's Psychology and Girls' Development*. Cambridge: Harvard University Press.

Brown, Wendy. 1995. *States of Injury: Power and Freedom in Late Modernity*. Princeton: Princeton University Press.

Bucholtz, Mary, A. C. Liang, and Laurel Sutton, eds. 1999. *Reinventing Identities: The Gendered Self in Discourse*. New York: Oxford University Press.

Buker, Eloise. 1999. *Talking Feminist Politics: Conversations on Law, Science, and the Postmodern*. Lanham, Md.: Rowman and Littlefield.

Butler, Judith. 1990. *Gender Trouble*. New York: Routledge.

———. 1993. *Bodies That Matter*. New York. Routledge.

———. 1997a. *Excitable Speech: A Politics of the Performative*. New York: Routledge.

———. 1997b. *The Psychic Life of Power*. Stanford: Stanford University Press.

Butler, Judith, Ernesto Laclau, and Slavoj Žižek. 2000. *Contingency, Hegemony, Universality: Contemporary Dialogues on the Left*. London: Verso.

Cahn, Naomi. 1992. "The Looseness of Legal Language: The Reasonable Woman Standard in Theory and Practice." *Cornell Law Review* 77:1398–446.

Calmore, John. 1995. "Critical Race Theory, Archie Shepp, and Fire Music: Securing an Authentic Intellectual Life in a Multicultural World." In *Critical Race Theory*, ed. Kimberle Crenshaw et al., 315–29. New York: Free Press.

Caminero-Santangelo, Marta. 1998. *The Madwoman Can't Speak: Or Why Insanity Is Not Subversive*. Ithaca: Cornell University Press.

Capps, Lisa. 1999. "Constructing the Irrational Woman." In *Reinventing Identities*, ed. Mary Bucholz et al., 83–100. New York: Oxford University Press.

Carens, Joseph. 2000. *Culture, Citizenship, and Community: A Contextual Exploration of Justice as Evenhandedness*. Oxford: Oxford University Press.

Chodorow, Nancy. 1978. *The Reproduction of Mothering*. Berkeley and Los Angeles: University of California Press.

———. 1999. *The Power of Feeling: Personal Meaning in Psychoanalysis, Gender, and Culture*. New Haven: Yale University Press.

Cohen, Jean, and Andrew Arato. 1992. *Civil Society and Political Theory*. Cambridge: MIT Press.

Connolly, William. 1991. *Identity/Difference: Democratic Negotiations of Political Paradox*. Ithaca: Cornell University Press.

Cornell, Drucilla. 1995. *The Imaginary Domain*. New York: Routledge.

Cott, Nancy. 2000. *Public Vows: A History of Marriage and the Nation*. Cambridge: Harvard University Press.

Curry-Johnson, Sonja. 1995. "Weaving an Identity Tapestry." In *Listen Up: Voices from the Next Feminist Generation*, ed. Barbara Findlen, 221–29. Seattle: Seal Press.

Dean, Jodi. 1996. *The Solidarity of Strangers: Feminism After Identity Politics*. Berkeley and Los Angeles: University of California Press.

———, ed. 2000. *Cultural Studies and Political Theory*. Ithaca: Cornell University Press.

de Beauvoir, Simone. 1972. *The Second Sex*. Harmondsworth, Middlesex: Penguin.

Deleuze, Gilles, and Felix Guattari. 1977. *Anti-Oedipus: Capitalism and Schizophrenia*. New York: Viking Press.

Deveaux, Monique. 2000. *Cultural Pluralism and Dilemmas of Justice*. Ithaca: Cornell University Press.

Dietz, Mary. 1992. "Context Is All: Feminism and Theories of Citizenship." In *Dimensions of Radical Democracy*, ed. Chantal Mouffe, 63–85. New York: Verso.

Di Stefano, Christine. 1991. *Configurations of Masculinity: A Feminist Perspective on Modern Political Theory*. Ithaca: Cornell University Press.

Donzelot, Jacques. 1979. *The Policing of Families*. Trans. R. Hurley. New York: Pantheon.

Eisenstein, Zillah. 1988. *The Female Body and the Law*. Berkeley and Los Angeles: University of California Press.

Elshtain, Jean Bethke. 1995. *Democracy on Trial*. New York: Basic Books.

Espiritu, Yen Le. 1992. *Asian American Panethnicity: Bridging Institutions and Identities*. Philadelphia: Temple University Press.

Ferguson, Kathy. 1993. *The Man Question*. Berkeley and Los Angeles: University of California Press.

Fineman, Martha. 1995. *The Neutered Mother, the Sexual Family, and Other Twentieth-Century Tragedies*. New York: Routledge.

Flathman, Richard. 1989. *Toward a Liberalism*. Ithaca: Cornell University Press.

———. 1992. *Willful Liberalism*. Ithaca: Cornell University Press.

Flax, Jane. 1990. *Thinking Fragments: Psychoanalysis, Feminism, and Postmodernism in the Contemporary West*. Berkeley and Los Angeles: University of California Press.

———. 1993. *Disputed Subjects: Essays on Psychoanalysis, Politics, and Philosophy*. New York: Routledge.

Forell, Caroline. 1994. "Essentialism, Empathy, and the Reasonable Woman." *University of Illinois Law Review* 94:769–817.

Forell, Caroline, and Donna Matthews. 2000. *A Law of Her Own: The Reasonable Woman as a Measure of Man*. New York: New York University Press.

Foucault, Michel. 1965. *Madness and Civilization*. New York: Pantheon.

———. 1977. *Language Counter-Memory, Practice*. Ithaca: Cornell University Press.

———. 1979. *Discipline and Punish*. New York: Vintage.

———. 1980a. *Herculine Barbin, Being the Recently Discovered Memoirs of a Nineteenth Century Hermaphrodite*. Trans. Richard McDougall. New York: Colophon.

———. 1980b. *The History of Sexuality*. Vol. 1. New York: Vintage.

———. 1980c. *Power/Knowledge*. New York: Pantheon.

———. 1983a. "On the Genealogy of Ethics: An Overview of Work in Progress." In *Michel Foucault: Beyond Structuralism and Hermeneutics*, ed. Hubert Dreyfus and Paul Rabinow, 229–52. 2d ed. Chicago: University of Chicago Press.

———. 1983b. "The Subject and Power." In *Michel Foucault: Beyond Structuralism and Hermeneutics*, ed. Hubert Dreyfus and Paul Rabinow, 208–26. 2d ed. Chicago: University of Chicago Press.

———. 1984. *The Foucault Reader*. Ed. Paul Rabinow. New York: Random House.

———. 1988a. *Politics, Philosophy, Culture: Interviews and Other Writings, 1977–1984*. New York: Routledge.

———. 1988b. *Technologies of the Self: A Seminar with Michel Foucault*. Ed. Luther Martin et al. Amherst: University of Massachusetts Press.

———. 1991. "Governmentality." In *The Foucault Effect*, ed. Graham Burchell et al., 87–104. Chicago: University of Chicago Press.

Fowlkes, Diane. 1997. "Moving from Feminist Identity Politics to Coalition Politics

Through a Materialist Standpoint of Intersubjectivity in Gloria Anzaldua's *Borderlands/La Frontera: The New Mestiza.*" Hypatia 12 (2): 105–24.

Fraser, Nancy. 1997. *Justice Interruptus: Critical Reflections on the "Postsocialist" Condition.* New York: Routledge.

Frug, Mary. 1995. "A Postmodern Feminist Legal Manifesto." In *Feminist Legal Theory,* ed. Frances Olsen, 491–521. New York: New York University Press.

Frye, Marilyn. 1983. *The Politics of Reality.* Freedom, Calif.: Crossings Press.

Galston, William. 2002. *Liberal Pluralism: The Implications of Value Pluralism for Political Theory and Practice.* New York: Cambridge University Press.

Gatens, Moira. 1996. *Imaginary Bodies: Ethics, Power, and Corporeality.* New York: Routlege.

Gilligan, Carol. 1982. *In a Different Voice.* Cambridge: Harvard University Press.

Gilligan, Carol, Nona Lyons, and Trudy Hanmer, eds. 1990. *Making Connections.* Cambridge, Mass.: Harvard University Press.

Glass, James M. 1993. *Shattered Selves: Multiple Personality in a Postmodern World.* Ithaca: Cornell University Press.

Glazer, Nathan. 1997. *We Are All Multiculturalists Now.* Cambridge: Harvard University Press.

Grosz, Elizabeth. 1994. *Volatile Bodies: Toward a Corporeal Feminism.* Bloomington: Indiana University Press.

Habermas, Jürgen. 1979. *Communication and the Evolution of Society.* Trans. Thomas McCarthy. Boston: Beacon Press.

———. 1992. *Postmetaphysical Thinking.* Cambridge: MIT Press.

———. 1998. *The Inclusion of the Other: Studies in Political Theory.* Cambridge: MIT Press.

Hampshire, Stuart. 2000. *Justice Is Conflict.* Princeton: Princeton University Press.

Hartsock, Nancy. 1983. *Money, Sex, and Power.* New York: Longman.

Hekman, Susan. 1995. *Moral Voices/Moral Selves.* University Park: Penn State Press.

———. 1999. *The Future of Differences.* Cambridge: Polity.

Heyes, Cressida. 2000. *Line Drawings: Defining Women Through Feminist Practice.* Ithaca: Cornell University Press.

Hirschmann, Nancy. 1992. *Rethinking Obligation: A Feminist Method for Political Theory.* Ithaca: Cornell University Press.

———. 1996. "Revisioning Freedom: Relationship, Context, and the Politics of Empowerment." In *Revisioning the Political,* ed. Nancy Hirschmann and Christine Di Stefano, 51–74. Boulder, Colo.: Westview.

Honig, Bonnie. 1992. "Toward an Agonistic Feminism: Hannah Arendt and the Politics of Identity." In *Feminists Theorize the Political,* ed. Judith Butler and Joan Scott, 215–35. New York: Routledge.

Honneth, Axel. 1992. "Integrity and Disrespect: Principles of a Conception of Morality Based on the Theory of Recognition." *Political Theory* 20 (2): 187–201.

———. 1995. *The Struggle for Recognition: The Moral Grammar of Social Conflicts.* Cambridge: Polity Press.

Hunter, Ian. 1996. "Assembling the School." In *Foucault and Political Reason,* ed. Andrew Barry et al.,143–66. Chicago: University of Chicago Press.

Iglesias, Elizabeth. 1997. "Structures of Subordination: Women of Color at the Intersection of Title VII and the NLRA." In *Critical Race Feminism,* ed. Adrien Wing, 317–32. New York: New York University Press.

Jack, Dana. 1991. *Silencing the Self: Depression and Women*. Cambridge: Harvard University Press.

Jordan, June. 1994. *Technical Difficulties*. Boston: Beacon Press.

Jordon, Judith, et al., eds. 1991. *Women's Growth in Connection*. New York: Guilford Press.

Kerber, Linda. 1998. *No Constitutional Right to Be Ladies: Women and the Obligations of Citizenship*. New York: Hill and Wang.

Kirk, Gwyn, and Margo Okazawa-Reg. 1997. *Women's Lives: Multicultural Perspectives*. Mountain View, Calif.: Mayfield.

Kruks, Sonia. 2001. *Retrieving Experience: Subjectivity and Recognition in Feminist Politics*. Ithaca: Cornell University Press.

Kukathas, Chandran. 1992. "Are There Any Cultural Rights?" *Political Theory* 20 (1): 105–39.

———. 1998. "Liberalism and Multiculturalism." *Political Theory* 26 (5): 686–99.

Kymlicka, Will. 1989. *Liberalism, Community, and Culture*. Oxford: Clarendon Press.

———. 1995. *Multicultural Citizenship: A Liberal Theory of Minority Rights*. Oxford: Clarendon Press.

Larmore, Charles. 1987. *Patterns of Moral Complexity*. Cambridge: Cambridge University Press.

Lawrence, Charles. 1995. "The Id, the Ego, and Equal Protection Reckoning with Unconscious Racism." In *Critical Race Theory*, ed. Kimberle Crenshaw et al., 235–57. New York: Free Press.

Layton, Lynne. 1998. *Who's That Boy? Who's That Girl? Clinical Practice Meets Postmodern Gender Theory*. Northvale, N.J.: Jason Aronson.

Lerner, Gerda. 1986. *The Creation of Patriarchy*. New York: Oxford University Press.

Lorde, Audre. 1984. "Age, Race, Class, and Sex: Women Redefining Difference." In *Sister Outsider*. Trumansburg, N.Y.: Crossing Press.

Lugones, Maria. 1987. "Playfulness, "World"—Traveling, and Loving Perception." *Hypatia* 2 (2): 3–20.

Lyotard, Jean-François. 1984. *The Postmodern Condition: A Report on Knowledge*. Minneapolis: University of Minnesota Press.

MacCannell, Juliet. 2000. *The Hysteric's Guide to the Future Female Subject*. Minneapolis: University of Minnesota Press.

McClure, Kirstie. 1992. "On the Subject of Rights: Pluralism, Plurality, and Political Identity." In *Dimensions of Radical Democracy*, ed. Chantal Mouffe, 108–27. London: Verso.

McNay, Lois. 2000. *Gendered Agency: Reconfiguring the Subject in Feminist Social Theory*. Oxford: Polity Press.

Marcus, Isabel, et al. 1995. "Feminist Discourse, Moral Values, and the Law—a Conversation." In *Feminist Legal Theory*, ed. Frances Olsen, 143–219. New York: New York University Press.

Matsuda, Mari. 1996. *Where Is Your Body? And Other Essays on Race, Gender, and the Law*. Boston: Beacon Press.

Matsuda, Mari, et al. 1993. *Words That Wound: Critical Race Theory, Assaultive Speech, and the First Amendment*. Boulder, Colo.: Westview.

Mead, George Herbert. 1959. *Mind, Self, and Society*. Chicago: University of Chicago Press.

Millett, Kate. 1970. *Sexual Politics*. New York: Doubleday.

Minow, Martha. 1990. *Making All the Difference: Inclusion, Exclusion, and American Law.* Ithaca: Cornell University Press.

———. 1997. *Not Only for Myself: Identity, Politics, and the Law.* New York: New Press.

Mitchell, Steven. 1988. *Relational Concepts in Psychoanalysis: An Integration.* Cambridge: Harvard University Press.

Murdoch, Iris. 1969. *The Nice and the Good.* Harmondsworth, Middlesex: Penguin.

———. 1970. *The Sovereignty of the Good.* London: Routledge.

Nelson, Hilde Lindemann. 2001. *Damaged Identities, Narrative Repair.* Ithaca: Cornell University Press.

Norton, Anne. 1993. *Republic of Signs: Liberal Theory and American Popular Culture.* Chicago: University of Chicago Press.

Nozick, Robert. 1981. *Philosophical Explanations.* Cambridge: Harvard University Press.

Nussbaum, Martha. 1999. *Sex and Social Justice.* New York: Oxford University Press.

———. 2000. *Women and Human Development.* New York: Cambridge.

Okin, Susan Moller. 1989. *Justice, Gender, and the Family.* New York: Basic Books.

———. 1999. *Is Multiculturalism Bad for Women?* Princeton: Princeton University Press.

Olsen, Frances. 1995. "Feminism and Critical Legal Theory." In *Feminist Legal Theory,* ed. Frances Olsen, 473–89. New York: New York University Press.

Ortega, Mariana. 2001. "'New Mestizas,' 'World-Traveler,' and 'Dasein': Phenomenology and the Multi-voiced, Multi-cultural Self." *Hypatia* 16 (3): 1–29.

Parekh, Bhikher. 2000. *Rethinking Multiculturalism.* Cambridge: Harvard University Press.

Pateman, Carole. 1988. *The Sexual Contract.* Stanford: Stanford University Press.

———. 1989. *The Disorder of Women.* Cambridge: Polity.

Phelan, Shane. 1989. *Identity Politics.* Philadelphia: Temple University Press.

———. 1994. *Getting Specific: Postmodern Lesbian Politics.* Minneapolis: University of Minnesota Press.

———. 1997. "(Be)coming Out: Lesbian Identity and Politics." In *Feminism and the New Democracy,* ed. Jodi Dean, 124–45. London: Sage.

———. 2001. *Sexual Strangers: Gays, Lesbians, and Dilemmas of Citizenship.* Philadelphia: Temple University Press.

Post, Robert, and Nancy Rosenblum. 2002. Introduction to *Civil Society and Government,* ed. Nancy Rosenblum and Robert Post, 1–25. Princeton: Princeton University Press.

Rawls, John. 1971. *A Theory of Justice.* Cambridge: Harvard University Press.

———. 1985. "Justice as Fairness: Political Not Metaphysical." *Philosophy and Public Affairs* 14 (3): 223–51.

———. 1993. *Political Liberalism.* New York: Columbia University Press.

———. 1999. *Collected Papers.* Ed. Samuel Freeman. Cambridge: Harvard University Press.

Riley, Denise. 1988. *"Am I That Name?" Feminism and the Category of "Women" in History.* New York: Macmillan.

Rose, Nikolas. 1996. "Governing 'Advanced' Liberal Democracies." In *Foucault and Political Reason,* ed. Andrew Barry et al., 37–64. Chicago: University of Chicago Press.

Rosenblum, Nancy, and Robert Post, eds. 2002. *Civil Society and Government.* Princeton: Princeton University Press.

Rupp, Leila, and Verta Taylor. 1999. "Forging Feminist Identity in an International Movement: A Collective Identity Approach to Twentieth-Century Feminism." *Signs* 24 (2): 363–86.

Ryan, Barbara, ed. 2001. *Identity Politics in the Women's Movement.* New York: New York University Press.

Sanders, Lynn. 1997. "Against Deliberation." *Political Theory* 25 (3): 347–76.

Scott, Joan. 1995. "Multiculturalism and the Politics of Identity." In *The Identity in Question,* ed. John Rajchman, 3–12, 21–31. New York: Routledge.

Shachar, Ayelet. 2001. *Multicultural Jurisdictions: Cultural Differences and Women's Rights.* New York: Cambridge University Press.

Spelman, Elizabeth. 1988. *Inessential Woman: Problems of Exclusion in Feminist Thought.* Boston: Beacon Press.

Taylor, Charles. 1989. *Sources of the Self: The Making of the Modern Identity.* Cambridge: Harvard University Press.

———. 1994. *Multiculturalism and the Politics of Recognition: An Essay.* Princeton: Princeton University Press.

Taylor, Jill, Carol Gilligan, and Amy Sullivan. 1995. *Between Voice and Silence: Women and Girls, Race and Relationship.* Cambridge: Harvard University Press.

Torres, Lourdes. 1991. "The Construction of the Self in U.S. Latina Autobiographies." In *Third World Women and the Politics of Feminism,* ed. Chandra Mohanty, Ann Russo, and Lourdes Torres, 271–87. Bloomington: Indiana University Press.

Tully, James. 1995. *Strange Multiplicity: Constitutionalism in an Age of Diversity.* Cambridge: Cambridge University Press.

Walker, Margaret Urban. 1998. *Moral Understandings: A Feminist Study in Ethics.* New York: Routledge.

Weeks, Kathi. 1998. *Constituting Feminist Subjects.* Ithaca: Cornell University Press.

Weir, Allison. 1996. *Sacrificial Logics: Feminist Theory and the Critique of Identity.* New York: Routledge.

West, Cornel. 1995. "The New Cultural Politics of Difference." In *The Identity in Question,* ed. John Rajchman, 147–71. New York: Routledge.

West, Robin. 1991. "The Difference in Women's Hedonic Lives." In *At the Boundaries of Law: Feminism and Legal Theory,* ed. Martha Fineman and Nancy Thomadson. New York: Routledge.

Wildman, Stephanie. 2000. "Ending Male Privilege: Beyond the Reasonable Woman." *Michigan Law Review* 98 (6): 1797–821.

Williams, Patricia. 1997. "Spirit Murdering the Messenger: The Discourse of Finger Pointing as the Law's Response for Racism." In *Critical Race Feminism,* ed. Adrien Wing, 229–36. New York: New York University Press.

Winnicott, W. D. 1965. *The Maturation Process and the Facilitating Environment.* London: Hogarth.

———. 1975. *Through Paediatrics to Psycho-analysis.* New York: Basic Books.

Wittgenstein, Ludwig. 1958. *Philosophical Investigations.* New York: Macmillan.

———. 1960. *The Blue and Brown Books.* Oxford: Basil Blackwell.

Wolin, Sheldon. 1993. "Democracy, Difference, and Re-cognition." *Political Theory* 21 (3): 464–83.

Young, Iris Marion. 1989. "Polity and Group Difference: A Critique of the Ideal of Universal Citizenship." *Ethics* 99 (2): 250–74.

———. 1990. *Justice and the Politics of Difference*. Princeton: Princeton University Press.

———. 1994. "Gender as Seriality: Thinking About Women as a Social Collective." *Signs* 19 (3): 713–38.

———. 1996. "Communication and the Other: Beyond Deliberative Democracy." In *Democracy and Difference: Contesting the Boundaries of the Political*, ed. Seyla Benhabib, 120–35. Princeton: Princeton University Press.

———. 1997. *Intersecting Voices: Dilemmas of Gender, Political Philosophy, and Policy*. Princeton: Princeton University Press.

———. 2000. *Inclusion and Democracy*. New York: Oxford University Press.

INDEX